To Dad.

Lo … Lan.

YPRES 1917

YPRES 1917

A Personal Account

E. NORMAN GLADDEN

WILLIAM KIMBER · LONDON

First published in 1967 by
WILLIAM KIMBER AND CO. LIMITED
Godolphin House, 22a Queen Anne's Gate,
London SW1H 9AE

This edition reprinted 1977
ISBN 0 7183 0235 4

Printed in Great Britain by
Biddles Ltd., Guildford, Surrey

CONTENTS

Sketch maps of The Western Front and Ypres, based on the Official History of the War 1917, are on pages 6 and 7.

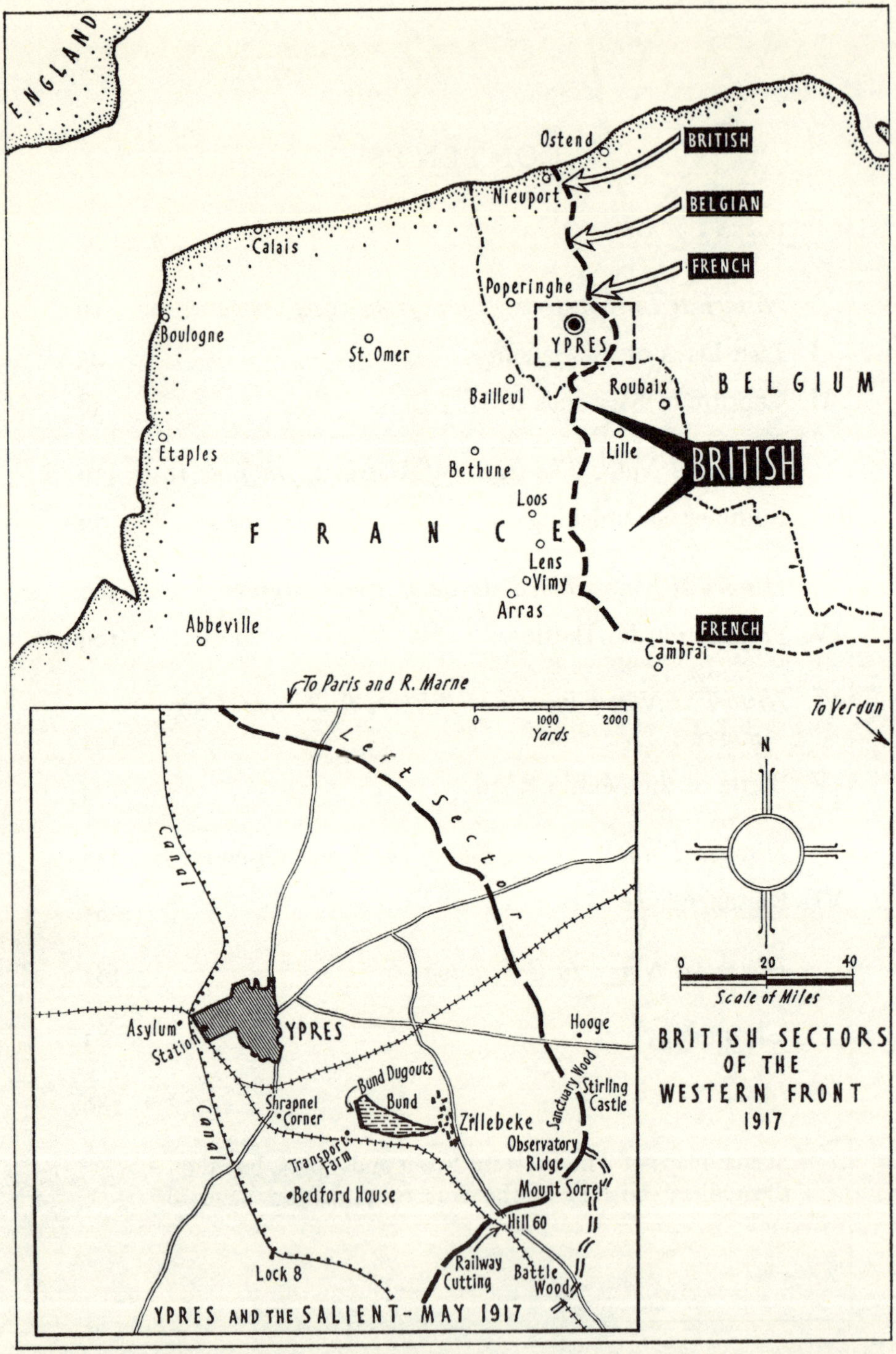

The Western Front, showing the relationship of the Ypres Salient to the main British front when the author joined his battalion in the line.

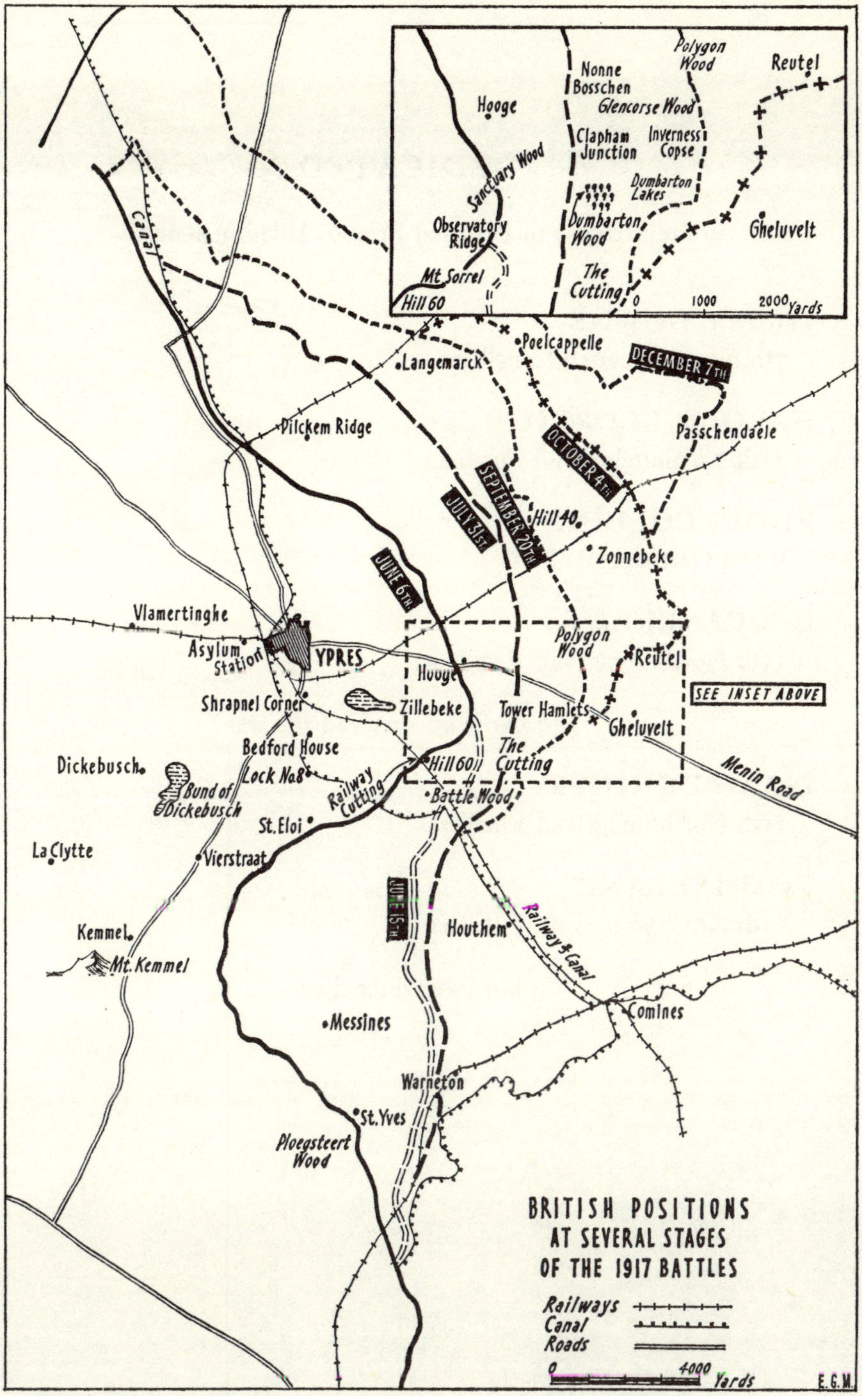

The successive lines forward of Ypres gained by the British from June to December 1917

DEDICATED

to the Memory of Personal Friends killed in action

JIMMY DOWNS
7th Northumberland Fusiliers

HAROLD ELDRED
11th Northumberland Fusiliers

EDDIE COLLINS
Royal Garrison Artillery

E. E. CANELLE
11th Northumberland Fusiliers

and two who survived the war

ISAAC DONIGER
11th Northumberland Fusiliers

TOM IRELAND
11th Northumberland Fusiliers

but have since died

PREFACE TO THE NEW EDITION

As explained in the original Preface, *Ypres 1917* is the middle section of a personal narrative, entitled *Full Pack*, based upon a diary kept during my army service from May 1916 to February 1919. It was the first part to be published, in 1967. The other two parts have since appeared. The final part, covering my experiences on the Italian Front during the last year of the war, was published in 1971, under the title *Across the Piave*, in paperback by Her Majesty's Stationery Office on behalf of the Imperial War Museum: the early part, *The Somme, 1916*, was published in 1974, by the present publisher in similar format to the present volume.

The Somme 1916, certainly the most depressing of these accounts, deals with the closing, waterlogged and muddled, slogging stages of that epic battle, into which I was thrust, with barely four months training, among a company of badly hammered and disorganized Northumberland Fusiliers, who treated their new members with a shocking lack of sympathy and in astonishing contrast to the reception given to his draft by the author's new company of the same famed regiment in the Ypres Salient, as described in the present volume. Thus *The Somme 1916* and *Ypres 1917* constitute a more or less continuous account of one participant's experience of the two devastating Western Front battles of the Somme and Passchendaele during 1916–17.

Across the Piave, a continuance of my experiences on the very different Italian Front mainly during 1918, differs considerably from the two earlier parts in presenting a wider picture of the slower-moving war in that area and thus makes a modest historical contribution to the British Army's exploits on a front about which much less has been published and, presumably, of which fewer personal accounts have survived.

Faced with the opportunity to review my original text, I quickly concluded that there were two important omissions from the narrative: two matters taken for granted in my personal diary and not in fact mentioned by any of my over-generous critics—namely, the less serious question of soldiers' language, and the vitally important matter of religious belief.

Most of us in the forces fell into the habit of using foul language, but there were certainly words that I would not use in any circumstance, though we have today become acclimatized to some of them on stage, over the wireless and in the press. Under trench conditions there were good excuses for letting off steam by the use of the most vulgar expletives we could lay our tongues to, and fictional accounts have fairly represented this aspect of army life. There were taboos of course. In my experience it was particularly dangerous to call anyone a bastard, as reflecting upon his mother's honour. It was said, though I never saw it demonstrated, that even a sergeant instructor could be struck for doing so, without the aggrieved ranker earning the due penalty for striking a superior officer. If this was just a myth it undoubtedly had wide acceptance in my unit.

On the important question of religion, we were initially each assigned his religious category and many, including some who were not churchgoers, opted for 'Church of England' (C of E), which covered many shades of belief and, importantly from the army's viewpoint, facilitated our sorting out for church parade. I was not much of a churchgoer myself, but fully accepted Christian precepts as the proper way of life and gained a good deal of inspiration from the scriptures, particularly the New Testament. In fact there still survives a compact khaki-bound edition, on the cover of which is impressed the inverted red triangle, with *YMCA* superscription in black letters. This pocket size edition was presumably obtained at the Base in May 1917. On the inside cover Lord Roberts's Message to the Troops on 25th August 1914, is printed in letter form, while on the opposite sheet I had written '1917 On Active Service' with my signature, and directed it to my mother at the family address in Putney. The title page is missing and so is a small part of the final chapter of Revelations: otherwise the small book, evidently carried in the lining of my tunic, seems to have survived almost as well as its owner. Certain passages were marked in pencil.

I belonged to a generation inspired by Christian doctrine, by inveterate love of country, by generous pride of the great British Empire, still the promise of a developing brotherhood greater than any of a non-sectarian nature that had been known before or certainly since, despite the fine promise of the League of Nations and of its successor the United Nations. We were inspired, too, by the vital task of protecting our homes across the Channel from the older madness threshing its way relentlessly across the Continent.

The historian's vital problem is so to interpret the facts that still survive as to provide a true picture of the situation as it was at the time, in fact to enable the reader to put himself in the shoes of the earlier participants. Even in such a recent event as the Great War of 1914–18, of which abundant first-hand information is available, it becomes more and more difficult to do this as time draws out and the band of survivors rapidly dwindles. This difficulty was clearly demonstrated by a recent quite excellent BBC broadcast, which consisted almost entirely of reminiscences by survivors of the Battle of the Somme, strung together with a minimum of commentary. It was, however, the selection and the emphasis that did not quite ring true to at least one listener, who did not feel that the producer's conception of what it was like was completely in focus. A television programme at about the same time on the same subject, amply supported by original silent film extracts, gave a much more accurate impression.

Thus when I heard one of the survivors in the broadcast assert that, at the outset of the great battle, the authorities had stationed Military Police to shoot anyone who refused to go over the top, I felt that something had gone wrong. Such an idea was completely alien to the spirit of that army. In any case even had such an idea been projected, its realisation would have proved impossible under the conditions of the Somme battlefield.

The point was actually discussed and challenged by correspondents in *The Radio Times* (for the week 17–23 July 1976) and the producer confirmed that the statement was based upon the word of 'the General Commanding VIII Corps' who 'informed a number of Pals Battalion shortly before 1st July 1916 that if any soldiers hung back at the moment of attack there would be somebody waiting to shoot them'. If the programme's interpretation of this Blimpish approach were true, one could only conclude that the number of casualties among members of the Military Police from the German barrage must have been very high, which seems unlikely. I never saw a military policeman in the trenches, although this is not to say that they did not appear from time to time in the course of duty, possibly to escort back a delinquent who had been properly arrested for some misdemeanour.

Old-fashioned generals, not in tune with the spirit of the new armies, did of course sometimes chatter tactlessly. There are incidents in my three books which, taken out of context, could be quoted to support the existence of a special security force of the type attributed to the general and, specifically, I emphasize how the authorities at the Base drummed into newcomers the seriousness of the penalties imposed for dereliction of duty, but we knew all about this before we left our home camp and generally accepted it as a necessary precaution against the odd case of cowardice or sheer treachery. In any case the responsible officer or NCO on the spot had the authority, and would have known how, to deal with such a case. There were of course the shell-shocked Tommies, frightening sight, but no one in his right mind would have shot such an one for running away. In any case, in face of the actual situation in the line before an attack, it seems that the Military Police themselves would have been the most likely ones to run away, and I feel sure none of us would have been disposed to blame them.

One of the difficulties of correctly interpreting such reminiscences is that they are honestly believed by their retailers. We all heard the like at the time they were supposed to be happening, and some seemed so unlikely that we were immediately sceptical about them. Rumour was rife in the army, and in the absence of internal publicity, was seized upon with avidity. We were all inclined to believe what we heard, until a new rumour flooded in to replace it.

The truth is that each of those fighting men in all the armies on all the fronts experienced his own personal war which differed in its unique essence from those of all the others. This statement certainly applies to the three volumes of mine which I wrote as truly as I knew how, because I believed that anything else, though it might provide more stimulation to the reader, would make little contribution to the task of preserving even a small part of the multitudinous reality for posterity.

New Barnet, 1976 E. N. GLADDEN

PREFACE

This is a personal story of the First World War of 1914–18, or the Great War, as it was generally called. It is a plain account of the impact of one phase of that vast struggle, in which countless young men of many nations and races sacrificed their lives, upon one unimportant British citizen-soldier, a private in the Northumberland Fusiliers. It has to do with the experience of an infantryman at ground-level and is not in any way concerned with the responsibilities of leadership or the grand strategies and policies of captains and politicians, with whose histories the shelves of libraries are filled. Not that it is by any means the first of such personal stories or likely to be the last, so long as a single member of the dwindling band of participants survives. If any excuse be required for this further repetition, it may perhaps be found in the truth that every man involved in so vast and devastating an upheaval, though he shared the experience of everyman at war, also had an experience that was personal to him and unique, as every human is unique from his fellow.

At this stage, some half a century on, the genesis of this particular tale calls for some explanation. It is not a feat of memory, much less a work of imagination. All that is set down here happened and in the exact order of its recounting. The record began as a brief day-to-day diary—a task made difficult by army regulations and doubly difficult to the ranker whose facilities were always restricted. The miracle is that it survived, together with its writer to reinterpret it. This reinterpretation in extended form was undertaken in the years following the war, when the events and personalities still lived vividly in the author's mind. But it was clear at the time that such a diary contained too much repetitive detail for it to be suitable for publication. A poet could have made it otherwise, but then it was hardly a poet's experience and the war was far from being a poet's war, whatever the evidence to the contrary. Nevertheless it did provide the source of contributions to *Everyman at War* (Dent, 1930)—which was reprinted in *Vain Glory* (Cassell,

1937)—and to the second volume of *I Was There* (Amalgamated Press, 1938).

Subsequently, and from time to time, the diary was converted into narrative under the general title *Full Pack—A Private's War*, which covered in separate parts the three phases of the writer's experience on the Somme in 1916, in the Ypres Salient in 1917, and with the Italian Expeditionary Force in 1918. The present work, to be issued on the occasion of the fiftieth anniversary in 1967 of the Battle of Messines and Third Battle of Ypres, is the first complete section of the work to appear in print.

Since the reader cannot be expected to be an expert in the wider context of events which gave meaning to the writer's experience at the time, and indeed of certain vital matters of which he himself was not then aware, it is intended, by means of an historical introduction and of factual linking passages between the several chapters, to provide the necessary background.* But first let me say something about my personal situation at the time the narrative opens.

* * *

I had left school in 1913 upon passing a modest Civil Service examination which had given me the coveted prospect of a life career at a time when security in employment accrued to few. When the war came out of the blue in 1914 I shared with the majority a complete unawareness of the great impact which this event was to have upon all our lives, if indeed we were to preserve those lives! My seventeenth birthday happened to coincide with the 4th August on which Britain declared war on Germany, and I saw no reason to anticipate being called upon to take any part in the fighting, which to me was clearly a task for grown robust men.

I was fit enough, but not robust, an office worker rather than a land man, a confirmed patriot certainly, but not confused by the prevailing romanticism which made so many dream of glory. My particular imagination, reinforced by the great flood of war journalism at the time, left me with few illusions as to

* Acknowledgement is due to the Controller, Her Majesty's Stationery Office, for permission to quote certain paragraphs from *The Official History of the War* within these historical notes.

what war was really like. Examining some of that current reportage today, I cannot understand how anyone could have been unaware of the truth. Added to this was a natural horror of the hardships and unavoidable intimacies of army life, which would have held me back in any case.

I did not therefore need the edict of my employer, His Majesty's Postmaster-General, on the cessation of recruitment of officials once the initial excitements had been allowed to work themselves out, to convince me that my proper duty was to carry on with my job until such time as my King and Country should decide that my services were required in a military capacity. As things turned out, the demands of the armed forces began to outrun the resources made available by the voluntary system of recruitment, which we all supported at the time, and later in 1915 the so-called Derby Scheme was introduced, under which all who were prepared to serve were invited to enlist for one day and be returned to civil employment—on loan, as it were, by the military authorities—there to be classified according to marital status and age and to be recalled to the colours according to group, as and when needed. The Post Office now having lifted its ban on recruitment, I enlisted as a Derby's man in December, donned my crown-emblazoned khaki armlet, and was allocated to Group I for Single Men to await call up at the age of nineteen.

My call came early in May 1916, three months ahead of my nineteenth birthday. Even then I was passed fit only for home service, for high standards were still being maintained, and the medical man toyed with the notion of putting me back for a few months. This inclination received no encouragement from me, for I wanted a firm decision to be reached. I was allocated to home service with the Hertfordshire Regiment and joined its 2nd Battalion in the stables at Newmarket, proceeding subsequently with them to camp on Killinghall Moor, Harrogate.

In May there was no official design to turn me into a fighting man within four months. Many whom I knew had already been in training at home since the early months of the war, and even the military authorities, with all their faults, would not have been so foolish as to plan the impossible. But events were already materialising to cause them actually to achieve just this. The great build-up for the forthcoming Somme offensive was bound to put a great strain upon the grand Kitchener's Army which had been so long in training, but the unanticipated human cost of the disastrous attack of the 1st July and of the subsequent period of relentless attrition changed the whole situation. I remember how, when we first went to Harrogate, the officers and N.C.O.s were actively bemoaning the prospect of not reaching the front before it was all over! In the event I was upgraded medically almost on a weekly schedule, taught to obey orders and handle arms in double-quick time, and then assigned to a draft for the Northumberland Fusiliers, under a new arrangement whereby home-based units no longer continued to feed only their own fighting units at the front. I crossed to France on 30th August, which was pretty good going if not a record, spent a bare fortnight in hectic training in the notorious Bull Ring at Étaples and, via a brief attachment to an Entrenching Battalion in the Ypres sector of the front, reached the Somme battlefield towards the end of September, when the campaign was already bogging itself down in the autumn mud. My draft joined the 7th Battalion Northumberland Fusiliers in the 50th Territorial Division in time to take part in the capture of Le Sars.

The situation in France was then unspeakably depressing. Even our arrival at the base camp had been welcomed by a group of jeering nondescript Tommies, no doubt down from the line, as 'more for the slaughter-house', while arrangements on the Somme front were chaotic. The battle lines were fluid in more senses than one, mere ditches for the main part with little cover and hardly any shelter from the elements; the service organisation in support was primitive in the extreme. At one period, which included towards the end participation in a major attack in the Butte de Warlencourt area in November, the company spent twenty-six days in the forward zones, with a minimum of shelter, practically no cooked food, hardly any washing or changing facilities, and depending upon drying out only when the days and nights happened to be fine.

To add to our discomforts the new draft was received by the battalion without ceremony or any sort of induction. We were absorbed by our company like bodies being sucked down into a morass and made to feel that we had no rights of any sort. We had difficulty in obtaining our just rations, poor as they were, were put on all working parties—from which the old hands honestly thought they had earned exemption—and even in the trenches found ourselves without shelter because we had not yet learned the ropes. The N.C.O.s and officers never appeared unless there was some mission to perform, and for once in my life I learned what it would be like in a society without authority in which the ordinary man determined his own privileges according to his own scale of values.

This was my worst period in the army, a time when depression effectually completed the task which the enemy had legitimately in hand. As if by a miracle I escaped death or even wounding, but the lackadaisical conditions eventually led to my temporary release when the prevailing wetness brought on the peculiar army complaint known as trench feet. This should have released me from the final battle, for instructions for my clearance had actually been issued, but this was ignored; with even more prolonged neglect, the resulting septic ulcers on both feet at long last led to my precipitate evacuation down the line to reach No. 6 General Hospital at Rouen shortly after 2 a.m. on Christmas Day 1916. No treasure cave of Araby could have appeared so wondrous to my eyes as the gaily-bedecked ward on that most memorable of Christmas mornings.

The subsequent interlude in Blighty, commencing with lavish Welsh kindness in hospitals at Cardiff and Bridgend, and continuing with an all-too-brief home leave, led to the most inhospitable of camps at the Northumberland Fusilier base depot at Catterick in Yorkshire. By April I could use my feet as well as ever, and march, fix bayonets and slope arms with the best, and so was adjudged ready for the next round, knowing the worst before it began and feeling the wheel of fate already turning against me.

As if to confirm my worst apprehensions, but this time in terms of another's suffering, I was never to forget an incident on one of our final parades when the draft was being tidied up for departure. Harold Eldred, a young recently married recruit, just discharged from hospital following a serious illness and still looking weak and insecure, was brought to the parade ground to join the draft. This was to be his first journey overseas. A gap had to be filled and this was the way the problem was neatly solved. The minion of the inhuman machine who did this thing, and happily saved himself a sleepless night, could not have had the least twinge of conscience about it in Biblical terms, but to me he was none the less a minion of the Devil, more sinful than any who had broken one of the ten commandments or been taken *in flagrante delicto*.

Thus it was that I, No. 292669 of the Northumberland Fusiliers, together with Harold Eldred, my new friend, and many other reluctant comrades, to the strains of 'Cock o' th' North', left Catterick station on 1st May 1917 for the front. Fortunately for me, although the twice-told tale was to have some of the characteristics I had already experienced—some with enhanced agony and sadness—this new experience was to hold many surprises and to restore my shaken faith in humanity. But for the time the grim shadow of the Somme weighed upon my soul and filled me with an active resentment against the incompetence of my fellow men, although, never for one moment did I challenge the necessity of the task we had in hand nor harbour the least doubt that things would come out right in the end.

Ypres, noted medieval city, was to discover a new fame during the First World War. At the beginning of hostilities in 1914 the French armies, swinging the enemy line back from the Marne, had literally closed a door, through which the great German strategist von Schlieffen had planned to open up the Channel ports and Paris to the German horde. The small band of British professionals on the Allied left flank made Ypres the latch to that door, which it was to be a vital task of the British Expeditionary Force to keep closed throughout the campaign.

German patrols had reached the outskirts of the city in October 1914, but had failed to maintain a foothold. A major German thrust towards Calais had developed into the First Battle of Ypres, with the comparatively weak British force poised along the high ground about Passchendaele and Messines. On their left the Allied flank to the sea was held by the remains of the Belgian Army, strengthened by a French force. The British left held firm, but the right was forced back from the Messines Ridge, creating in its first form 'The Salient', to which history has given an immortal name. In this area, stretching at the time from between four and five miles from the city, there emerged a fortified zone around the city's perimeter which was to grow into one of the strongest positions on the Western Front.

Not that the Germans were content to leave things as they were. Many hard-fought battles were staged round the fiery wall. Indeed, as soon as spring had come in 1915 the enemy launched another major offensive. For the first time in war the Germans used gas, brought up to the front in cylinders; their foes were totally unprepared for what was considered a major declension from the accepted rules of war, yet, despite the great advantage of this unheroic surprise, the Salient—though further restricted—continued to hold fast. On the left, the line was now consolidated within a couple of miles of the city. In their new positions the Germans could enjoy almost complete observation over the British lines and use them as a veritable anvil, against which our troops were to be hammered mercilessly until the great release came with the Battle of Messines early in June 1917.

In fact, with the Second Battle of Ypres the Germans had to accept stalemate at this key-point and rest content, during the remainder of 1915 and throughout 1916, with regarding it as a place for profitable attrition. In this policy, it should be added, they were strongly aided by the British custom of keeping the pot boiling at the front, by raids and stratagems, designed by high authority to maintain the offensive spirit of the troops. While there was undoubtedly something to be said for this policy, it was not one that the troops themselves whole-heartedly accepted!

All this time the war was continuing on many fronts, not only in France and Flanders, but in many parts of the world, against a mightily armed enemy effectively consolidated on internal lines which ensured that, to him at least, the conflict was one and undivided. As indeed it was. The struggle was one struggle between opposing ideals; the story was one story, even if the main participants were often at cross-purposes, at any rate on the Allies' side. Every battle had its repercussions on every other battle, even if the most percipient strategists at the time, and the best-informed historians since, have not always been able clearly to discern just what those repercussions were.

Among the campaigns of 1916, the battles at Verdun and on the Somme, both struggles of epic magnitude, were undoubtedly of major significance in shaping the events with which this present work is primarily concerned. At Verdun, where the offensive had been taken by the Germans on 21st February, the thrust was frustrated by the superhuman efforts of their French opponents, who came to regard the defence of this key-point as a matter of supreme national honour. This battle, one of the bloodiest of a bloody war, was to continue to the end of the year at a cost of some 300,000 casualties to each of the protagonists. Relief had come to the French with the launching of the great Somme offensive by the British on 1st July, as indeed was the aim, but again the cost was terrible and the new offensive's main objectives were to prove as elusive as ever. After the flower of Kitchener's New Army had been sacrificed to the bullets of the German machine-guns on that bright summer morning this battle, too, was to continue, as it seemed endlessly, until brought to a standstill in the autumn mud.

On these two battlefields of 1916 was war of an intensity and doggedness such as had never been reached before, and the youth of three historic European nations were sacrificed senselessly to nebulous concepts of honour, though it has to be admitted that few of the participants saw it that way. Never surely was there greater justification of the Latin proverb: Quos Deus vult perdere, prius dementat. *The scene was set for 1917.*

The new year, like every other during the Great War, began on the Western Front with renewed hope, however unpromising might be the outlook almost everywhere else. All the armies had suffered grievously during the earlier campaigns—Russians, Austrians and Italians as well as the three Western protagonists—none more than the French, who, although poised for a further massive effort, were nearer to breaking-point than was at the time realised. The Germans, of course, were feeling the strain, but were buoyed up by hopes for the success of their intensified U-boat campaign of 'sink at sight'. This, it is true, added the United States to their formidable list of enemies, a potential giant whose advent in April 1917, welcome as it was to the Allies, was not for some time to assume that degree of importance in the contemporary mind, including the minds of the men in the trenches, that it has since come to assume. There is a continuing tendency to reinterpret the past in terms of the present world and it is naturally not easy for us today to comprehend the feelings of those who had been bearing the burden of war for nearly three years towards a nation whose leader had boasted of 'being too proud to fight'. The Germans certainly expected to finish the job long before sufficient American power could be deployed, and tested, on the battlefields of the West—and their calculations were not to prove so very far out.

Early British thrusts on the Somme front in 1917 gave a clear foretaste of the war of continuing attrition that the British Commander, Sir Douglas Haig, held firmly in prospect. These activities did, during March, bring forward a planned withdrawal by the Germans on the Arras-Somme front to their newly constructed and massively fortified Siegfried Line, generally known to the Allies as the Hindenburg Line. This somewhat disconcerting retreat to prepared positions, leaving the main Somme objectives of 1916 at last comfortably in Allied hands, was supplemented quickly on 9th April by a full-scale British thrust upon the Vimy Ridge, a strongly defended German position at the point where the new Hindenburg Line hinged on to the old line to the north of Arras. After a brilliant initial success in which the Ridge was captured, the previous pattern was repeated. The Germans dug in their heels and the drive forward was halted at a high cost to both sides.

Meanwhile, France's new military leader, General Nivelle, had replaced General Joffre. With the backing of the politicians, but against the better judgement of the military leaders, he had been authorised to carry out a grandiose plan to deliver a crushing blow on the Rheims-Soissons front. Based upon the apparent lessons of the war to date, the aim was to break the line and at long last to administer the coup de grâce *to the invader. Nivelle was supremely confident, but the Germans countered first with a strategic retreat to straighten a particularly difficult sector of the line, then followed this up with a massive machine-gun fire concentrated on dispositions, information of which they had actually captured from the French. The Germans were again able to bring to a standstill the truly heroic efforts of the French troops, who had entered the battle with high hopes skilfully influenced by Nivelle's propaganda. In the eyes of the ordinary Frenchman this further military failure assumed the proportions of a most grievous disaster with repercussions that were both widespread and devastating. The morale of our much-tried ally was, for the time being, shattered.*

Concurrently with this major disaster at the front, supply ships to beleagured Britain were being sunk in increasing numbers, while, far away to the east, the shadow of a great army, acclaimed in the enthusiasms of 1914 as 'the Russian Steamroller', was fading into chaos and revolution.

The scene was most certainly set for the great struggle which was to be known in history as the Third Battle of Ypres, a vast holding operation, although unrecognized as such by the majority of its participants. In some ways, with Britain's back to the wall, this was the equivalent in the annals of war to the Battle of Britain (1940) in the later struggle between the same protagonists.

* * *

The Third Battle of Ypres consists of a series of major actions which are variously named in the history-books. It was part of a grand plan of Sir Douglas Haig's to free the Channel coast of Belgium and to turn the enemy's flank, hitherto securely anchored on the North Sea with only a small sector of Belgium beyond the Yser left to the Allies. Such a campaign had already been planned in 1916, but discarded in favour of the Somme operations of that year.

The first phase of the new Ypres battle came to fruition with the Battle of Messines on 7th June 1917, virtually a one-day operation, although it was not officially regarded as closed until the 14th of the month. It was a necessary preliminary to the designed break out from the coast. In fact, an Allied attack on their coastal positions was frustrated by the Germans at Nieuport on 10th July and thus the main operations were to be concentrated athwart the Ypres-Menin road, thrusting towards the open country beyond the Passchendaele Ridge. Thanks to the far-sighted German defensive system, based largely upon the holding of difficult, often waterlogged, ground by a system of well-placed concrete strong-points and helped to no small extent by the vicissitudes of the weather, the massive thrust was to be almost immediately converted into an endless slogging match.

Officially the Third Battle of Ypres began on 31st July with the Battle of Pilckem Ridge, which lasted until 2nd August. The next stage, known as the Battle of Langemarck, began on 16th August, only to be overtaken by shocking weather and to come to a standstill on the third day. After a breather for the redeployment of forces, the campaign continued late in September with a series of fierce engagements known severally as the Battle of Menin Road, from 20th to 25th September; the Battle of Polygon Wood, from 26th September to 3rd October; the Battle of Broodseinde, on 4th October; and the Battle of Poelcapelle, on 9th October. By this time the open-country objectives were becoming tantalisingly visible to the men engaged, but at the same time the advance was losing its final momentum in a terrain in comparison with which the morass of the Somme now appeared as a kids' playground. Here followed what were perhaps the most awful struggles of all, a grappling on the borders of victory and defeat by two teeth-set opponents, which the Teuton won on points, a Pyrrhic victory if ever there was one. These final stages of the campaign were to be known, from 12th October, as the First Battle of Passchendaele, and from the 26th October to the end on 10th November as the Second Battle of Passchendaele.

The Official History regards these two Passchendaele battles as part of Third Ypres, although it leaves the preliminary Messines attack its own distinctive title. In many accounts Passchendaele, such was its notoriety, retains a distinct status, while other writers, with geographical inaccuracy, give the title to the entire campaign. The official nomenclature seems as good as any, though no shuffling of labels will alter the fact that the Battle of the Salient throughout 1917 was one coherent campaign which lasted almost unceasingly for five weary months. Verdun, Somme, Third Ypres: such battles as these in their grim, prolonged intensity, there never had been in the world before.

The closest study of the facts, of the strategies and plans of the proponents, of the statistics of power and of human sacrifice, of the heroism as well as the failures of men, must still leave serious doubts as to why events worked out just as they did. It is possible that the clue to the problem rests finally in the experience of the numberless small men who were involved in the mighty upheaval.

CHAPTER I

LAST DAYS OF THE SALIENT

On 2nd May 1917 we breakfasted in the boarding-houses alongside the jetty at Folkestone within the area that had been divided off as a rest camp. Our excitement at having been allocated to these improvised billets spontaneously induced a rumour that we were to stay there a while; but by 9.30 a.m. we were aboard the transport ready to leave. It was a beautiful morning. A bright May sun shone down upon a calm blue sea and caused the white cliffs of Dover to glitter in a friendly way as we moved out into the Channel. Two dark destroyers guarded our flanks, while a small Admiralty airship manoeuvred to and fro overhead, looking out for menacing undersea shapes which would have been easily discernible from the air. I had a satisfying feeling that beyond the vacant horizons rode the remainder of the Royal Navy, preserving us from any enemy attack. It was a remarkable feat that so many armed men thus continued to be ferried across the narrow seas without loss.

Spring had come even to Boulogne, where the rest camp that night no longer seemed the forsaken place I had pictured to poor Eldred, who was feeling all the hopelessness of first leaving the homeland. I knew what to expect—or thought I did—and felt myself forearmed against an impossible future. It was like reading a book a second time, although, in place of faulty memory which often brings surprises to such an enterprise, the march of time had already brought unexpected differences in the plot that was for a second time unfolding. Indeed, in more senses than one there was little parallel between that first stormy crossing of August 1916 and this lovely day.

I had made up my mind to meet the future at least halfway. Forewarned was forearmed. I would suppress my natural diffidence and refuse to be put upon. My morale was boosted by the thought that I had qualified as an Old Soldier experienced in war, and I would let this be known. Moreover, I had the advantage of being able to use my experience, not only on my own selfish behalf but on that of another who was very much the tenderfoot and indeed deserved protection. I still rankled with a sense of injustice at the way Eldred had been pitchforked into active service, and these feelings went some way to lighten the burden of my own despair.

The following day, instead of taking the slow train to Étaples, we actually marched all the thirty kilometres, halting at the rest camp at Neufchatel for our midday meal. Even the base camp at Étaples wore a new look, although I could not clearly discern at the outset just where the main difference lay. Certainly, we had not to suffer the sarcasms of that depressing reception party, but perhaps the greatest difference was within myself. I was really a different man seeing the same scene differently.

Our Northumbrian depot had been moved away from the railhead, deeper into the bustling settlement. We were again in bell tents. The usual visits and parades followed, but it was on the first day at the initial medical parade that an incident occurred which suggested that official attitudes had changed little. The medical officer, a callow youth who could not have long passed through the schools, swept along the line rapidly, his staccato, unsympathetic questions drawing little response. His few replies were insulting and we boiled within ourselves. He came to an elderly member of the draft, a wounded warrior old enough to have been his father. The old soldier's face was pinched with illness, his body drooped forward and he had a limp. His first words were snapped short by the M.O., who, almost snarling, accused him of lead-swinging and asserted that he certainly should not miss the line. This professional paragon then made his victim, half naked, run up and down the hut, seeming to take a fiendish delight in the man's clear look of agony. The standing line murmured as though a breeze had passed through the hut, but none had the courage to show his disapprobation in more definite terms. These M.O.s no doubt had a lot to put up with and there may have been some excuse for the curtness and lack of sympathy which they so often displayed, for it is true that malingering was widespread and could easily have got out of hand, but this was the worst case I ever encountered and it made a deep impression upon us all. One wonders what happened to that particular lout in hero's clothing. No doubt he got through the war and grew up to become a respected member of a noble profession, and no doubt the healing hand of time will have masked with convenient forgetfulness the sheer wickedness of his actions at Étaples in 1917.

On the second night of our stay at the base the weather was so fine and warm that many of us left the crowded tents—sometimes containing as many as fifteen men—to sleep in the open. Each morning we rose at 5.30 to carry out intensive training at the Bull Ring, where there had also been numerous changes, but not in the depressing yesmanship of the Canaries,* buying with their souls a brief respite from that other hell.

It happened that on the very first day we carried out a programme in the built-up trench system which simulated visually so well the conditions at the front. But the important part that was missing had little to do with the appearance of things. Most of us now knew what the reality was like and this makebelieve no longer impressed. The training continued according to plan until the second half of the month. During this programme the only real novelty was our introduction to the new box respirator, which was without the least doubt a great advance in comfort and efficiency over the old flannel bag.

The atmosphere of the camp had lightened in several directions. Discipline was certainly less strict, and it was even said that passes were obtainable into the town. The dwellers of this temporary city amidst the dunes had become much more varied. There were many more nurses, V.A.D.s, female servers at the canteens, and so on. The morale of the base wallahs was being looked to, though perhaps not the morals. A full-scale cinema had been constructed, upon the placards of which Mary Pickford's image was emblazoned to cheer the exiled population. For those in the know there were other delights. The officers had their own impressive canteen and rumour spoke of rare goings on at night-time. Our ancient allies from Portugal had their own sector, their drab greenish-grey uniforms tempering the

* N.C.O.s and officers with experience in the line temporarily assigned to instructional duties at the base, so named from the broad yellow arm-band which they wore.

monotony of the khaki scene. But one had to admit that their lines were slack and dirty, their manners to any women who drew near execrable. Our boys were hardly plaster saints, but the presence of women always brought out the best in them, indicating an entirely different approach to the eternal female. In later years I was fortunate to meet the Portuguese in their own lovely country and to learn how poorly their troops at Étaples had represented their compatriots at home.

To be fair, I recollect a scene which showed the other side of the picture. One day we marched in the sunshine to the army laundry which had been improvised on the river bank opposite the sea-side township of Paris-Plage. Alongside the placid, somewhat characterless, estuary, the ugly army building, spurting steam from a regular Heath Robinson structure of pipes, supplied abundant hot water for washing our underclothes. On the far bank, against a frieze of pretty villas, a row of buxom Frenchwomen were using the stream, as is customary on the Continent, as a laundry. The boys who were awaiting their turn at the tubs whiled away the time by conducting a long-distance love-making across the waters, a love-making that left little to the imagination, much to the delight of our friendly hosts, who were safely protected from this horde of predatory males by the wide band of water!

Twice during our stay German planes flew high above the camp, harassed but apparently unimpeded by our gunfire. After a few days my fortitude began to weaken and the camp routine to become boring. We were not really being heavily pressed, but it was the lack of freedom that always depressed me. I did not wish to roam in the existing circumstances, but I wanted to feel that I could do so. And then, after a spell of wonderful sunshine, the weather broke, inundating the tents with cold driving rain. The moisture seeped into my rifle and I was awarded an hour's pack drill, which was duly carried out that evening. It was the sense of injustice that weighed upon me, for I had already learned that prison sentences really matter only in a free world.

The one shining goodness in this sojourn was my growing friendship with Eldred. We found that we thought alike and liked the same sort of things. We were both quiet, retiring souls, wanting nothing better than to be left alone. He told me about his home in Peckham, his parents who kept a pub there, and his dear wife, whom he had just married in haste and left in their care. I envied him this rare felicity, which gave him a particular prestige in my eyes. He was perhaps a little older than myself, though I do not strictly remember.

The base camp was like a vast cistern into and out of which men flowed like water, although at that particular period it was fast filling up. Another draft arrived from Catterick in which there were many whom we recognised. One day from the parade ground, under skies filled with cold dreary clouds, we witnessed the stately progress of a military funeral, taking its further contribution to the accidents cemetery whose roll of 'killed in action', mostly by mischance at the camp, grew steadily as the months passed. We took this as an unkind pointer to all our futures.

By this time our draft had divided into two well-defined groups—the 50th Divisioners and the rest. The majority, particularly those from the Tyneside, wished to rejoin the former, in which so many of their friends still served, but there were many—including Yorkshiremen, a few Londoners and, for obvious reasons, myself—who had no wish to follow them. When, on 18th May, we were ordered to stand by for the line, we were also informed that we were to join the 11th Battalion in the 23rd Division. This news made us jubilant, if only because the 50th Divisioners were so cast down!

* * *

The train took us as far as Abeele on the Belgian frontier, where we stayed for the night in the reinforcement camp. The distant rumble of the guns told us that we were nearing the battle line. Before leaving the next day our brigadier-general came out to speak to us informally and created a good impression. A Belgian boy did a roaring trade disposing of his entire stock of *Continental Daily Mails*, a news service which did not normally penetrate far into the fighting zone. The youth escaped with a good-humoured box in the ears for perpetrating his, no doubt, daily joke, of announcing 'a Great British Disaster', but the news-sheet itself contained nothing more startling than the stereotyped references to mismanagement at home and the reiterated statement that it was all quiet on the Western Front. In the line we were still dependent on the delayed news coming over in papers posted from home and for local news had to fall back to a large extent upon rumour. Such a situation is difficult to imagine in these later days of wireless.

A three-hour march, somewhat fatiguing in the hot sunshine, brought us up to the Brigade School, situated in a typical farm, consisting of two rows of buildings separated by a long court-yard. Our billet for the night was one of the barns. The guns were now much nearer and we knew that we were on the way to the Ypres Salient, which had seen so much hard fighting almost from the beginning of the war. Yet the surroundings here were calm and rural, the neat rectangular fields all carefully tilled, with here and there a miniature forest of hop-poles standing up in orderly lines. A peasant worked steadily not far away, while many of the buildings were still occupied by farm folk, women and children predominating. They sold us milk and evinced no surprise when one of the new-comers, eager to demonstrate his linguistic ability, asked for '*lait de cochon*'. Alongside the farm a light railway led towards the sound of battle and from time to time one of the toylike engines puffed lustily by, groaning under the strain of hauling a string of overloaded trucks, about which groups of Royal Engineers often hung like so many flies.

The following day we marched further forward. For a time the only signs of military occupation were the occasional water points, with their facilities for doctoring the water with chloride of lime. Then the whole scene changed and we were in the area of the reserve camps, where we soon found our new battalion. These camps consisted mainly of neatly ranged rows of smallish huts, each equipped with a central stove, which must have made it cosy even in the winter. Their names—such as Montreal, Ottawa, Toronto—suggested that the Canadians had passed this way. We were in Ottawa. Even in this area the neighbouring fields were still green. Here and there cottages were still occupied by Belgians who no doubt felt that their homes were no less homes though within easy range of enemy artillery. That this was a number one target area was clearly indicated by the numerous camouflaged emplacements of our heavy guns sited among the hutments.

We were first seen by our regimental sergeant-major, a youngish type who behaved humanly. He allocated us to the four companies, giving each an opportunity to go with friends. Eldred and I were assigned to No. 6 Platoon of 'B' Company. Immediately after dismissal we were served with tea. This friendly but efficient induction differed so much from my previous experience that I straightway began to look to the future with much less apprehension. Nor were these early impressions belied by the attitude of our new companions. I let them know of my previous experience and was immediately showered with questions about friends in the 50th Division and the depot battalion. I felt at once that I had been accepted. Our new unit was one of Kitchener's battalions, evidently a mixed crowd whose outlook lacked the parochial slant of the Territorial battalions. Everything around us looked shipshape and well managed. One felt at once that the men mattered.

The 23rd Division had left the Somme in the early autumn, after suffering heavy casualties, and had come to the Salient, where they had been fully occupied ever since, alternating between working parties and spells in the line, which, we were feelingly informed, were just hell. Despite this warning note I felt justified in reassuring Eldred, merely on the evidence of our friendly reception.

Not a hundred yards from the camp was situated a large, well-equipped Y.M.C.A. hut with a sales counter heavily stocked with tins of fruit and other delicacies, cakes and chocolate, and many items of the sort on which we were wont to spend our army pay. This institution also boasted a small library of up-to-date fiction which could be borrowed on the deposit of one franc a volume. I was pleasurably surprised to discover such an amenity in the forward areas. It was abundantly clear that this front was much better organised than the Somme had been.

Suspended above the camps, and extending to right and to left as far as the eye could reach, was a row of observation balloons straining at the ends of their cables like huge inflated sausages and looking grotesquely defenceless in their exposed eminence. They were the eyes of the army. Our observers, generally two of them, in the basket beneath, were watching the enemy's every movement. This typical frieze at the back of the battlefield soon became an accepted part of one's picture of the front. They struck me at once when I arrived in the Salient, although I do not remember having seen them on the Somme. Yet I feel they must have been there and that their absence in my recollection is a mere aberration of memory. At Ypres they had their counterparts away beyond the German trenches.

At 6 a.m. the following morning the hut door crashed open to the boisterous entry of the orderly sergeant, shouting: 'Show a leg, me lucky lads.' A number of our colleagues, who had only recently returned from working party at a place of fearful possibilities known as the Bund, cursed him roundly and turned over to continue their sleep. The rest of us dressed hurriedly and tumbled out to our ablutions.

Our induction during that day went with a swing. During the morning we were seen by the colonel, a swarthy taciturn type, with the medals of some eastern campaign on his tunic, and by the medical officer, both of whom seemed to be satisfied with the new draft. Then we were ordered to the tailors to have the battalion's distinguishing mark—a neat green cloth circle the size of a penny—sewed on to the upper part of each sleeve of our tunics. The afternoon found us in Poperinghe on a visit to the army baths. I came to this historic place as to an old friend whom I found sadly aged even in the few brief months since my first visit. There were more jagged gaps in the architecture, more military traffic in the streets and many fewer civilians anywhere. The war was rapidly getting the upper hand. Both Eldred and I had been warned to stand by for working party that evening. Our initiation was not to be long delayed!

G.S. wagons* quickly transported us from the camp, along the tree-lined cobbled road, and past the long bare wall of the Asylum into Ypres. It was with no little awe that I alighted among the grim ruins of that City of the Dead. As we assembled in the main square, surrounded by spectral shapes, we seemed to be almost encircled by the enemy lights that rose and fell above the low ridges commanding the town. It was a comparatively quiet night for our début. There was only the murmur of laden limbers streaming through the town and of burdened men flowing amidst the empty frames of former dwellings. At fre-

* The motorised general service wagons now widely used at the front.

quent intervals lights glimmered up from sandbagged cellars showing that the place had its dwellers even in day-time when every square foot was under enemy observation.

We left the city on foot through the ancient ramparts, whose substantial construction continued to defy the enemy shells. Here the lights seemed to be so close as to deny the possibility that all our field defences lay between the town and the ridge occupied by the Germans. In fact, there was more space than appeared in the deceptive darkness between us and the line, but it was one of the outstanding miracles of the war that our armies had been able to hold such a closely invested place. The price, of course, was high, but this was a key position, as the enemy recognised.

We soon discovered the deceptiveness of those distances, as we traversed the duckboard track winding across the broken ground to the dump at Zillebeke, which was the night's rendezvous. Occasionally we halted, without apparent reason, as night-moving troops often did. The atmosphere seemed electrified and I was filled with an almost tangible expectancy of evil. Shortly something was bound to happen! I experienced that all-embracing fear which I had so often felt on the Somme. I was literally consumed by a fatalistic desire to do something desperate to pierce the shroud by which we seemed to be divided from some awful truth.

The night was calm. There was little artillery activity. Only occasionally a gun fired from one side or the other; only occasionally a machine-gun rattled out evilly in front. My companions spoke in hushed voices, as though fearful of waking some sleeping monster against whom there was no defence. Nevertheless from all around came the muffled murmur of moving men, like waves lapping against a distant shore. And above the comparative silence, which it merely served to accentuate, rose the croaking of a multitude of frogs, rendered abnormally numerous by the inundations caused partly by design and partly by the shelling. I first mistook their loud rasping croaks for the crack of machine-guns and ignominiously lowered my head, though I doubt whether this reaction was noticed in the darkness. The frogs continued their symphony throughout the night. No doubt it was their strange unexpectedness against the unanticipated stillness of the battlefield that caused me to notice their gabble more pointedly that night than I was ever to again. The realisation that their croakings were not harbingers of death no doubt automatically relegated them to their proper niche in the Salient's economy!

The Very lights* mottled the ground with twisted shadows. I seemed to feel death stalking around. The ghosts from past battles, induced by the tales of our companions, assisted in building up the tension. But that night had its own secret which it kept from us. Nothing really happened. We collected trench frames and duckboards near Zillebeke for transport laboriously to a place known as H-Trench. We arrived back in camp at 5 a.m. Two hours later we were dragged out to test our box respirators at the gas chamber. Their effectiveness gave us confidence. Despite my tiredness I could not sleep during the day, although I already knew that another trip to the line was fixed for the same evening.

Our second working party was a much more lively occasion. Already when we reached the city our guns, camouflaged by the ruins, were engaged in a vigorous strafe.† Feeling our way forward among the brickwork, fierce gun-blasts unexpectedly lit up the skeleton buildings around us. The whole place was filled with grotesque shadows; stentorian shouts were raised by the gunners as they laid their charges; while the replying fire searched the ruins, scattering the shattered brickwork far and wide. We passed right through the zone of hellish activity, halting and stooping and hesitating and not knowing whether the concussions were from our own guns or enemy shells. Our nightmare progress brought us at last to the ramparts and across the canal into the forward zone, which was again comparatively quiet.

On our way back, the tracks into the town being subjected to shrapnel bursts which were always particularly frightening, our sergeant decided to make a detour by taking to the railway line. This brought us to the area of the railway station, which was

* British name for the rocket of the firework type which was fired from a special pistol to light up the lines at night. The Germans were such assiduous users of this warlike amenity that it was our custom to use it sparingly and to leave it to the enemy to provide normal nocturnal illumination with his 'lights' or 'rockets', as we indiscriminately called them.

† This German word 'to punish' was widely used both literally as a verb and for 'a bombardment'.

being subjected to a steady bombardment with heavy 'coalboxes'. No doubt the Germans were hoping to catch troop concentrations there, but, except for the grotesque shape of the gasometer and a tangled mass of metal, there was nothing to be seen. The last train to Ypres had run some time during the previous autumn. Until then the railway had been the regular means of transport into the town, and the enemy must have been indulgent, for the railhead was under full observation. On that occasion, however, a group of troops had been caught when detraining. Needless to say, we did not tarry in this unwholesome place.

On our arrival in camp it was discovered that we had suffered casualties and two of our number were missing. This was hardly surprising in light of the great confusion during the shelling of the tracks. The Salient had assumed a very different guise on this second night, but we were being introduced to its tricks and whims by easy stages and still had much to learn. When Eldred and I discovered that we had been allocated to working party for the third night in succession we began to wonder whether we should be able to stand the pace—not that we had any choice in the matter.

On this third night the routine was again varied. The old-fashioned char-a-bancs which were used as transport on this occasion deposited us on the near side of the town, where we had to collect trench-mortar bombs for transportation to a store behind the reserve trenches. These particular missiles were shaped like heavy metal footballs with a stalk in the form of a tube, by which we carried them over the shoulder. They were weighty and awkward objects to transport, for after a short time the tube began to bear painfully into one's flesh. To make matters worse this was one of the enemy's active nights. His gun-flashes lit up the horizon behind the screen of dancing lights, and the widely scattered shell-bursts suggested that he was probing for something. It was only natural that we should imagine it was for our insignificant selves!

While halting at a spot by Jackson's Dump a member of the group, to soothe his nerves—of course, against the strictest orders—lit a cigarette. So great was his desire—and so obscured his judgement—that he was prepared, in that place of all places, to risk not only his own but all our lives! Though the match was shielded in his cupped hands the flame glowed through his fingers like a beacon in the darkness of the night. A howl of indignation went up, as the file hurriedly moved off. The riposte was not long delayed. An enemy machine-gun began to traverse accurately across the track, scattering us like rabbits to the shelter of a ditch, but not before two of our company lay writhing in agony with bullets in the lower part of their bodies. The firing ceased and, after the wounded had been tended, we moved forward again in an advanced state of nerves. Every shadow in the near distance seemed to harbour the threat of death. Needless to say, the thoughtless one was not hurt! Not that his action was at all exceptional. Under the stresses of the battlefield a smoker could become desperate enough to be willing to risk anything for his normal means of release from tension. I formed the view that the habit of smoking had merely increased the capacity for such tensions and that the smoker's nerves in war were not any steadier than those of the rest of us.

This particular incident made it abundantly clear to me what great advantages the enemy derived from occupying the high ground beyond the town. His fire, both machine-gun and artillery, could be accurately directed upon selected map references with the practical certainty of finding a target. Bursts of machine-gun fire continued intermittently throughout the night, keeping us all in a high state of nerves. At the forward dump, having deposited our loads, we rested a while. All around us in stacks covered with flimsy camouflage were accumulations of trench-mortar shells, boxes of bombs, rifle-grenades and other types of ammunition looming up like humps out of the darkness. They seemed to invite enemy fire, but must have been so situated as to be masked from observation.

As we waited, coloured flares went up from the line somewhere ahead: a rattle of musketry indicated a heightening of activity in that sector and immediately the guns on both sides joined in a general bombardment. Shells began to hunt perilously near the dump and for a second time that night the working party scattered in all directions. I found myself crouching behind one of the humps, my vivid imagination running riot over the probable results of a direct hit upon the stack. It was one of those moments when the continuing fear rose to a crescendo of terror such as no words can possibly convey to those who have not experienced it. Fortunately, the storm quickly subsided. The dump escaped again and, except for the occasional rifle-shot, the troubled sector returned to the state of jumpiness by which the Salient that night was obsessed.

We stumbled back tired and nervy, our numbers considerably dwindled, not from casualties but from absences through scattering. Not that all the absentees had actually lost their way. I had already begun to discover that there was in the company a group of practised lead-swingers who knew how to evade the effort and had no compunction in allowing others to bear more than their fair shares of the common task. In fact, they were proud of their cleverness and made no secret of their subterfuges.

Prominent among this group were the real old soldiers who had served as regulars before the war. They knew the ropes and the lay of the land. Thus on this particular occasion most of the missing had already reached the assembly point before the transport took us back to camp. The prince of these lead-swingers was well known, from the vigorous and pointed quips of his closer companions, and I remember him well. He was a gaunt Irishman, much older than most of us, who had served in India and had no intention of taking this new sort of soldiering more seriously than he was compelled to. His limbs of steel and high reputation as the company's best boxer shielded him effectively from internal wrath, while for the authorities he had little respect and no fears. He reckoned that he would be as well off in clink as anywhere else, but usually managed to dodge that sort of retribution. For a quiet life, the N.C.O.s ignored his absence, technically a serious offence under army regulations. Despite the esssential meanness of his conduct, his polished effectiveness in doing what many of us would have liked to do earned him a respect that was probably conducive to his continuing in his accepted role. He had a reputation to maintain!

It was now the 25th May. Our three-day intensive nocturnal apprenticeship had provided us with a most effective introduction to the Salient, whose widely advertised reputation for evil had been made a living reality to us. We did not know it then, and there were those among us who, alas, were never to know, that these were the Salient's last days in its most restricted form. This spot where the troops of the Empire were then fighting, and would continue to fight almost to the end of the war, one of their greatest battles was approaching its hour of greatest crisis. Ringed in by the enemy's concrete and steel, unprecedented power was now flowing into the curved hoop of constant tension and death. The time of uneasy equilibrium was nearing its end. With such pent-up forces something was bound to break. A winter's efforts were not designed to bring repose to ourselves any more than to the enemy, who was probably as confident as ever in his ability to continue to hammer us against the anvil we had elected to construct, rather than surrender such an important position. Harold Eldred and I, and all those shadowy others from many a thousand homes, were poised on the threshold of something big. Yet despite all the hectic activity which we were now witnessing and the allusive conversations of our new companions, touching upon so many recent events and neighbouring places in the line, I cannot recollect that their cumulative effect was to impress my mind with anything near the truth.

I could only compare this place with the Somme, where I knew a great battle had been fought, which, nevertheless, had left in my mind no clear impression of anything purposeful happening. There one was acted upon without experiencing the impression of actually participating. The Salient, as I already knew, was quite different. Here at the very gates of an exceptional hell, a hell much more concentrated in its mechanical deadliness than the Somme, we were encamped in comparative safety and unexpected comfort. The keynote of the reserve areas was orderliness. Everywhere there was movement, but movement without haste, movement with apparent purpose, as though every step had been carefully charted—as apparently it had. Here was a neatly patterned reservoir of troops and supplies to feed the fistlike battle front. The saving grace of this evil place—wherein it was such a contrast to the Somme—rested in the ease with which its defenders could get away from its deadliness. The troops involved were given, as a general policy, only small doses of its hell. It was easy, provided one survived, to get right out of the maw of death. Efficient organisation had clearly been the secret of the front's persistence. The Germans, having originally failed to close the trap, were constantly faced with active, rested troops who had not merely to be watched but to be constantly restrained from springing outwards, as it were. The strain on the enemy must have been almost as great as upon us, despite his strategic superiority.

At this period there were gaps in our company's Lewis-gun sections and volunteers were invited. This type of approach was adopted because these light machine-gun teams were considered a sort of suicide club, though I think this was grossly exaggerated. True or not, there was no eager response to the appeal. I had no difficulty in persuading Harold to join me in volunteering, and we were duly assigned to our own platoon team.* I had been influenced towards this action largely by my experience of the privileged position of the specialist in my previous unit. As it turned out, while the several types of specialist were still regarded as important, any special privileges in our new battalion were confined strictly to the needs of the particular job.

That night we were not called to the Salient. I slept the deep recuperative sleep of youth, reinforced by the accumulated fatigue of the three preceding nights. The camp and all the world around us looked very different the next day, an indefinable film seeming to have been pulled aside to disclose much detail hitherto taken for granted. It was good to be alive. Yet, if our untired eyes discerned the immediate present so much more clearly and even optimistically, our less-encumbered minds rendered our natural apprehensions about the future even more acute.

This day of enhanced acuteness was a good one to be introduced to our fellow gunners and to be provided with beginners' instruction from the little red book, which began by portentously informing us that our new weapon was not a gun but an automatic rifle. The few lessons I had received almost casually at Harrogate the previous summer served me in good stead, and the intricacies of the 'cocking handle' and the 'cartridge guide spring' were not completely incomprehensible, despite a natural lack of interest in things mechanical on my part.

Our section leader, Corporal Goffee, whose two stripes indicated that he also acted as second-in-command of the company's

* Each of the four companies had four Lewis guns, one to each platoon.

four Lewis-gun teams, was an old soldier who had seen service in India. In his early thirties, he was a good-humoured cockney who was universally liked, but yet had sufficient authority and more than sufficient competence to make a good N.C.O. All his team were youngsters in their early twenties. Our Number One was Westgarth, an amateur runner of no mean ability, and the others were Sutton, a reserved, gentlemanly type who had little to say for himself; Hardcastle, a tall, spare but somewhat loquacious Yorkshireman who worked on the railways in civil life; Golightly, dogmatic and inclined to worry over the least trifle; and Weatherall, a short good-natured sort who took everything as it came and seemed to worry about nothing. The two latter and Westgarth were coal-miners. Altogether they were a likeable group, who made us feel at home straight away. It was soon evident that, except for Sutton, who was inclined to keep to himself, they were continually bickering among themselves and indulging in horse-play, but equally they were to remain close friends the whole time that events left them together. I was always to be *persona grata* in the section, though remaining outside the inner 'chumship' circle. The contrast of this new settling in with my previous experience on the Somme was so startling, as well as welcome, that I took every opportunity to impress Eldred with our good fortune, though not having had that other experience he found it difficult, I know, to overcome his own sense of the injustice of his lot, an attitude with which I was in complete sympathy.

That night again found us in the forward areas, on this occasion pushing loaded trolleys up to Sanctuary Wood, that scene of many fiendish battles and whose very name filled me with awe. The once-flourishing woodland, now a poor travesty of splintered tree-trunks notching so low along the horizon as to afford little cover, fringed along our front line. This is the wood that almost every reader must have seen depicted in modernist paintings of the First World War, in a form that provides the atmosphere as well as the mere shape of a horror that could be more easily felt than described.

Our destination was a point but a few yards behind the trenches, whose movements were distinctly audible. Occasionally a bullet broke into the night and echoed in hollow flight through the wood: more frequently an enemy rocket, bursting above us, bathed the maimed stumps in a bluish haze, giving the whole scene a touch of dreamlike unreality. At such moments we instinctively halted our trolley and stood transfixed in grotesque attitudes until the light had faded. Yet it was a comparatively quiet night, that magnified the clatter of the trolleys, which seemed loud enough to awaken the dead and filled us with anticipatory fears until we were free to turn round and trundle our unloaded vehicles back to the dump. The journey back was undertaken thankfully, but speeded substantially by the enemy, who chose this moment to worry the track with desultory shellfire.

The following day was Sunday, which would have been more comfortable had it not been my turn for mess orderly duties.* That night we rejoiced in not having a working party, but our joy was short-lived. For four or five hours during the night our artillery carried out a nagging bombardment, to which the enemy made a measured reply. Shells fell all over the back areas, many in our vicinity, and at one time the gas alarm was sounded. That was the only time I came to consciousness, and then only briefly. I was so tired that the threat of death could not keep me awake. By all reports it was a most hectic night in the camps. Reports of losses and damage were coming in from all directions, though we had been lucky in our battalion. Elsewhere shells had fallen amidst the transports, killing many horses, which were always sad targets, tethered as they were. The gas hut was holed and a direct hit on the Y.M.C.A. damaged the piano!

During the morning orders came for us to pack up for a spell in the line. The huts had to be cleaned and left shipshape for our successors. Rations had been satisfactory, much better and more abundant than I had ever experienced on the Somme. There had even been a surplus of jam, a commodity which in times of shortage we had learned to eat with almost anything. The ledge above the hut door was loaded with unopened tins—which we could not possibly carry with us—not merely of the proverbial plum and apple, but such blends from Australia as quince and peach, as well as home-made marmalade, which was less popular. A member of the platoon bundled a good supply

* Normally my belonging to the Lewis-gun team would release me from this communal chore.

into a sandbag with the intention of 'flogging' it at a surviving estaminet where he knew business could be done.

Eldred and I took the opportunity to write letters at the Y.M.C.A. and to purchase a few necessaries that would be useful in the trenches. A padre came over to chat pleasantly with us and comment upon our tired looks, which nevertheless must have been much improved since the day before, and to wish us good luck in the line. Eldred tried a glass of beer. As something of a connoisseur, he liked this little better than the local wine, which he thought very poor stuff. I did not mind the wine at any time, but was completely allergic to the beer, and have been ever since. This was the moment for us to exchange home addresses—in case. And now, remembering my woeful failure over Jimmy Downs to whose next of kin I'd failed to write, I made a mental resolve that I would not break faith again.

* * *

At 7.30 on that evening of 28th May we left in motor-lorries for Ypres. It was still daylight as we sped into the straight alongside the broken façade of the Asylum, and I could not help thinking grimly that the destruction of this building was symbolical of the whole process of war. We were immediately spotted by the enemy balloons hanging low over the horizon beyond the city. This stretch of road was an obvious target, registered to the inch by the spotters. The barrage fell around us as if a button had been pressed. As the lorries careered forward frantically shells burst around without warning, for the noise of the motors drowned their approaching whine. Our lorry swayed: flying debris spattered down on to the hood and against the woodwork. We lurched round a recently made shell-hole and narrowly avoided running off the road on to the waste ground below. With a final mad rush, which swept us from our feet into a heap at the bottom of the vehicle, the lorry drew up dead in the main square opposite the damaged Cloth Hall, which I then saw clearly for the first time. Two of the lorries had been hit, and it was difficult to see why this particular risk had been accepted by the authorities. After such a shake-up, we paid little attention to the desultory strafe that was being carried out as a matter of routine against the battered carcass of Ypres town.

We took the track to the Bund dug-outs, which were to be our billets, in reserve, for the next few days. As soon as we had dumped our packs we were ordered forward on a carrying party, from which we returned about midnight, when I was among those immediately detailed by a N.C.O. who was organising a ration party to Transport Farm not far away. The battalion mules had reached the farm—now reduced to a few broken walls—and it was important that they should be unloaded and turned round without delay, for this was a hot-shop and serious losses could be sustained by transport caught immobilised on such a mission. Our arrival at the farm almost synchronised with the next enemy strafe, the bursting shells falling around and about, lighting up the shattered brickwork and surrounding tree-stumps. The party scattered and the mules began to stampede. There could have been a disaster had not our C.Q.M.S.* Fail taken decisive action, instructing his men to quieten the mules and to issue the bags indiscriminately, and adding that it was every man for himself in getting the rations back to the dug-outs. Above all we were to avoid bunching under fire.

My bags contained bread, bulky but light. I felt that for once I was doing something really worth while, but this hardly conquered my fear. The path lay across open ground below the dug-outs and I had gone only a few paces when a nicely timed salvo of shrapnel shells burst overhead. I ran and, out of breath, had gained the slight shelter of the steeper slope before the next salvo arrived. Then it seemed that all hell had been let loose across the broken ground and I marvelled that I was still alive. With the first promise of a lull I rushed frantically towards the deeper shadow of the dug-outs, subsiding, exhausted and wondering, in the friendly safety of the sandbags that reinforced the entrances. The rations were delivered.

It seemed to me then, as it seems to me still in distant retrospect, a miracle that anyone could survive in that terrible place. The threat of death, sudden and horrible, was ever present. Its signs were all too visible even in the night, the air saturated with the sickening smell of putrescence. Wherever one's eye pierced the curtain of darkness a hastily dug grave with its improvised cross became visible or the dark corpse of some recent tragedy

* Company Quartermaster-Sergeant, a warrant officer ranking.

awaiting under its shroud of sacking the moment for its hurried interment. In the daylight these graves could be seen dotted about wherever there might be some shelter, usually alongside the track. Not far away, under an embankment where the trains once ran and near the road leading out from the Lille Gate, hard by a similar reserve position known as the Railway Dug-outs, there was a cemetery in the making which was designed to be the eventual assembly place for these temporary burials. Unfortunately these dug-outs were a favoured target for the enemy guns. Shells fell continually into the graveyard, disinterring the rotting corpses, spreading the nauseating odour far and wide as the breeze listed. The mixing of hot steel with cold earth and putrid human flesh into a ghoulish pudding went on day after day.

All this and much more I was to learn in the immediate future. For the moment my one need was to rest, to sleep and to forget about dying. I found a vacant corner at the back of the dug-out and began to make myself some sort of couch upon the floor. A distracted corporal at this moment entered the dug-out and straightway ordered me back to the farm for a further trip. I escaped only through the spontaneous assurances of Private Berry, a man of outspoken manner and caustic tongue who had been one of the recent carrying party, that I had already made the journey and a suggestion that there were plenty of others who should take a turn. This incident further impressed upon my mind the great difference between this and my previous unit, where no one ever bothered to speak up for a new member in this way. Yet I found myself too unsettled now to do more than doze until I heard that the last man had returned.

I awoke to shouts of 'Breakfast up', with sunshine slanting through the dug-out opening. Hot bacon and tea were served at the cookhouse dug-out towards the end of the embankment: this was luxury indeed. Next door there was a small Y.M.C.A., the closest I had seen to the line. If it had little for sale, its presence was at least comforting!

I was pleasurably surprised. So this was the famous Bund, about which there had been so much talk back in camp, the place of many meetings and incidents during the company's journeyings in the Salient. It was a highly dangerous spot which skilful engineering had made quite hospitable and relatively safe. The Bund of Zillebeke was a small lake shaped roughly like a leg of mutton with the wider end towards Ypres and away from both curves of the line. In the steep bank, in the lee of the lake, a line of sandbagged dug-outs had been constructed in such a way that the shells which missed the bank above slithered over to burst on the flats below. A burst had to be very accurately aimed to hit the track which passed alongside the dug-outs. Each of the latter consisted of a hooped corrugated-iron enclosure set well into the bank, piled high with sandbags, and large enough to shelter about eighteen men. The entrances were gained by a short flight of steps, also massively sandbagged. Safety was only relative, for the enemy knew that there was activity behind the lake and well-timed shrapnel shells were often so aimed as to catch careless loungers in the dug-out entrances. We kept religiously to the duckboard track and no wider movement was possible during the day.

As I sat on that first afternoon by the dug-out opening I was filled with wonder at the scene around me and had an awesome feeling that I was at the very hub of history. My dislike of present discomforts and fears for the future, strong as they were, were yet not powerful enough to still an inquiring mind that discovered both a sense of unworthiness and a mastering pride at being there just at that point of time. I looked around me, almost furtively, to discover whether any of my companions were feeling the same way, but if they were they did not show it. They were either busy with small mundane matters or drugging their boredom by snatching some of the sleep they would surely not experience during the night ahead.

Before my eyes spread the martyred city, whose resistant walls still shaped the remains into the semblance of a dwelling-place of men. A concourse of shattered buildings clustered in the middle distance, with here and there a broken chimney stack or a decapitated church spire jutting a little above the rest. There was no human movement. The place looked as though it had been abandoned half-finished to the elements. But this was only the superficial appearance of things, for every now and then, here and there, a shell burst among the rubble, demonstrating clearly the cause of the city's dire condition.

Every day for weeks and months the enemy had been directing shells, some of them very heavy shells, on to this hapless target. It was a miracle that anything resembling a town remained and I felt amazed as I watched on that afternoon, a helpless witness of war's impersonal ravishing.

At one point, on the very edge of Ypres, a shell hit something highly combustible, causing flames and smoke to well up and die down intermittently for some time. Even this hardly affected the brooding quiet that seemed to dominate the scene. The bombardment was both inhuman and inconsequential. No one seemed—at that distance at any rate—to be taking any notice. I knew full well that every inch of the ground was under direct enemy observation. To walk there in daylight meant almost instant death. Not until nightfall would the area return to life and teem with the hectic activities of modern warfare. On the other hand, closer in, under the cover of our embankment, there were many signs of life. Officers and men passed back and forth on missions, clear only to themselves or to those who issued their orders way back at headquarters out of the reach of artillery.

It was thus that the Salient revealed itself to me, explaining much that I had failed to understand during the dark nights that had gone before.

That night we went forward along the left-hand side of the lake to begin digging a new communication trench across the flats. It was one of those quiet nights when the crack of an enemy light seemed to resound throughout the Salient, and even the few shells that sailed exchangefully in opposite directions forgot to screech. We had worked on steadily into the early hours before something unusual happened. It was high upon the horizon ahead of us, where the Left Sector, as the northern flank of the Salient was called, showed clearly how the line ran, that a massive flash unexpectedly lit up the entire landscape. Some seconds elapsed before the earth under our feet trembled like a vast drum, while from the same quarter the rattle of machine-gun and rifle-fire welled up to a crescendo and then died away as quickly as it had begun. A mine had been fired. In the quietness that followed my brain was filled with lurid pictures of the horror of being involved in such a cataclysm, than which I could imagine nothing more awful. Yet the night itself refused to be perturbed and in the ensuing silence, broken only by the metallic searchings of our picks and shovels against the resistant earth, there was absolutely nothing to suggest that a tragedy had just occurred.

During the afternoon of the following day the Bund was subjected to a sudden whirlwind bombardment, mainly with shrapnel. The enemy was well on his target and we finished up with twelve casualties, some of which looked pretty bad. All were got speedily away, their departure being blessed with our good wishes, enviously given, for there were few who would not have opted for the lesser evil of the wounded men—after the event. That night we went forward again to complete our previous task. On the way we became involved in a heavy strafe at a spot by the lake where new gun positions were under construction.

With the last daylight of May still reigning over a quiet Salient we left the Bund, under the cover of the communication trench, for the front line on Hill 60, long famed for its defence in the early attacks and still reputed to be one of the hottest parts of our line. Our route was sheltered until we had to cross a section where the trench practically disappeared and a board by the remains of a hedge warned us to beware of the sniper. Bending low, we quickly came to a modest hump, which, I was surprised to discover, was the famous hill. But its true prominence was reduced by the dusk and it was not really surprising that such a low eminence, which nevertheless dominated the surrounding flat with all the further ridge in the hands of the enemy, should have been a key-point whose occupation was vital to our holding of the Salient.

A deep passage led into the rubble, marked at the entrance by a large red cross which denoted the vicinity of an advanced dressing-station. Here also were the field kitchens and other company offices. Skirting the mound, we entered the railway cutting on the branch line to Comines. Here we gazed upon a scene of desolation that was beyond description, a world quite of its own, with the smell of explosives hanging in the night air as though we had arrived—to our good fortune—in the lull of a bombardment which was practically continuous. A sharp turn down the embankment and we were almost immediately mounting a steep communication trench leading across the hill itself. It was reassuring to feel the steep sides of the trench about one!

'B' Company took over the second-line trench, our No. 6 Platoon occupying the first bay. On our arrival this trench, with its heavily sandbagged sides and well-placed fire-steps, looked very like one of those model positions we had seen at the base—quite different from anything I had witnessed on the Somme. But in the searching light of the following morning things were to look very different: the trench had been badly battered and constantly rebuilt, the newly placed sandbags looking like patches in a shabby but neatly repaired coat. In most places the trench was too wide for safety. At the rear the ground could be seen sloping steeply towards the top of the hill: in front visibility was limited to the range of a periscope. To look over during the day meant instant death. At night, however, under the almost continuous glare of the German flares one could see fairly widely, but with little precision. The world out in front was peopled by dark shadows that seemed ever on the point of moving. There was a waste of shell-holes skewered foolishly with unconnected barbed-wire pickets, a mess of broken cans tossed untidily out of the trench with, in the immediate foreground, a dirty half-buried mess-tin to focus the whole picture. It was a just setting for death. Further forward the two front lines ran together so close as to be almost untenable. During the day strong-points only were held, while at night patrols crawled about. Ours was therefore virtually the main defence position. Just below our post, dug into the opposite wall, was a well-used latrine which added its stink to the normal stench of war.

The earth about us trembled with the throb of machinery as the pumps down below chugged unceasingly to keep the marsh waters out of the galleries by which the hill was now honeycombed. The marvel of this underground fortress was only gradually unfolded as we saw new sections of it and were able to piece together some coherent picture of its ramifications and of what was going on underneath the battlefield. Our Lewis-gun post was situated at the head of a sap, the opening of which was blanketed against gas. A steep stair led straight down into a wide passage, shored up with heavy timbers and lined with sleeping-bunks arranged in two layers. Each bunk had a base of wire netting which was frequently broken, so that it was wise to choose one's cot carefully. The galleries were lit by electric light. Although the air was not stagnant, there was a heavy odour of humanity and a sickly smell of things rotting, some of which rose from the waste water running along channels under the bunks.

Our time throughout the twenty-four hours was divided into duty spells—two hours on and four off. Much of the time we spent below reading and dozing. To sleep was not easy; for there was a continuous coming and going along the narrow gangway between the bunks. One's slumbers were frequently broken by a rap from a swinging rifle butt or dig in the ribs from a bayonet scabbard, or some other projecting part of the passer's equipment. A shower of dry dust, dislodged by the vibration, trickled down intermittently between the timbers, possibly into one's ear, and sleep vanished in an outburst of blasphemy. Worse than all else, the place was literally alive. I had already, a day or two earlier, seen a solitary advance-guard on my jacket. Now the lice were massing for the attack. There were half a dozen crawling on the sleeve of Eldred's coat. He discovered them with all the horror of one who first experiences the filth. I was merely perturbed. It had to come sooner or later: and now we had another pastime for our idle moments.

Down below we wore a cap comforter—a double-knitted wool rectangle that could be easily converted into a cap which pulled down over one's ears. Above ground we had to wear steel helmets: gone were the days when those who preferred the old cloth cap could please themselves. The trouble about the underground shelters was that they made us feel too safe. It took a special effort to go out even into the comparative safety of the trench. Thus protection from death was paid for by a weakening of morale: yet it was a price that had to be paid, since without the defence works Hill 60 could not have been held.

I was completely intimidated by the mere appearance of things on that awful hill. I could remember nothing on the Somme that gave such a dramatic picture of war's utter ghastliness. Statically for months and months the two sides had faced each other, pounding the earth, smashing and rebuilding defence works with little change of position. It was as though death itself permeated the very air, needing no further impulse to continue the work that had been going on since some indefinite yesterday. Yet all was still outside. Our first night had passed quietly, except for an occasional bullet, zipping across the ground and burying itself in a sandbag of the parados behind us. The comparative quiet lasted into the next day, although there was shelling away to the left as well as to the right of our sector.

While on sentry during the afternoon I watched with interest—and apprehension—one of our heavy trench mortars firing from an emplacement by the Railway Cutting. Its heavy 'footballs' sailed in a wobbling arc over No-man's-land to fall with a heavy crash upon the enemy line. One could see a number of these heavy missiles in the air at the same time, giving the impression that they were being literally pumped out of the projector. After each explosion the iron stalk of the bomb boomeranged back with a moaning wail, usually to fall not far from our position. The trench mortar was an effective weapon developed for just this type of warfare. We also had the lighter Stokes canisters, which were so mobile, and the heavy flying pigs that I had seen down at the dump, fearsome objects which would no doubt wreak havoc among the dug-outs. I had been told about the enemy's heavy '*minnewerfer*',* frightening missiles which one could see in the air—and try to dodge! That afternoon we expected some such reply, but none came. The extraordinary silence continued.

It was on the evening of the 3rd June, shortly after stand-to, that the illusion of tranquillity was ruthlessly shattered. I happened to be on sentry with Sutton: he stood on the fire-step scanning the ground out in front, while I stood within reach to challenge any movements along the trench. The rest of the team had gone down into the sap. Except for the slight glimmers that came from below through chinks in the gas blanket our world was empty and desolate. I had a strange unearthly feeling; for this was something different from what I had experienced before. Enemy rockets lit up the ghostly landscape almost continuously, causing the sandbags around us to glitter in their reflected light. This was the scene that had so often been pictured in the current journals and has since been hung in many exhibitions of paint-

* Usually shortened to 'Minnies'. The correct term '*Minen-werfer*' actually means mine-thrower or trench mortar.

ings, a world that existed only during those dying years, a world never really comprehended except by those who were there. It was a world not merely to be seen and smelt, but to be felt both in the marrow of one's bones and in the terror of one's soul.

Suddenly the situation changed dramatically: fury took over from mere intimidation. Over beyond the enemy lines the skies lit up with the simultaneous flashes of many guns, whose reports were audible before the breaking of the storm. I sensed the flood of shells tearing inevitably towards our position, a marked spot on all that grim battlefront. The first arrivals were not far from the parapet and immediately the noise of explosion became continuous as one burst merged into the next. No chance shooting this: they knew their target and meant to hit it. Obviously this was a reply to the trench-mortar strafe, or so I thought, my mind searching for some logic in the event. But, of course, I knew nothing of the greater events that were pending and I was not capable of seeing the happening in its true perspective.

Sutton remained calmly on the step, his head just above the level of the parapet, watching—motionless and silent. I pressed close to the sandbags, wondering why the trench had been made so wide. Shell-bursts were close, blasting fumes and earth into the air and blotting out all visibility. We survived those first moments because none of the early shells happened to register a direct hit on our section of trench.

Pulling the dug-out blanket hastily aside Corporal Goffee shouted for us to come down. I passed the message to Sutton but, although he was only a few feet away, he appeared not to hear. I pulled his greatcoat, yet he continued to stand as though hypnotised at his post with his eyes still fixed upon No-man's-land. Fear now gripped me and I rushed into the sap, halting breathlessly beside the corporal, with the rest of the team standing to on the steps immediately below. The corporal continued to shout his order to the sentry, who still took no notice. His inactivity was inexplicable and I cannot explain it even now. It may be that the suddenness of the onslaught had deprived him of all initiative, or it is possible that an acute sense of duty made him feel that his presence at the post was so necessary that this was an occasion when orders should be ignored.

The inevitable happened. A shell burst right on top of the sap, sending us reeling down the stairway. A shrill cry came from the trench and we dragged Sutton down to safety straight into the hands of the stretcher-bearers who were at hand ready for such an eventuality. His head was covered with blood; an arm dangled limply from his side as he was borne away. Fortunately the well-equipped dressing-station was quite near and could be reached through the galleries. A wounded man's chances of survival were therefore good, and I believe that our team-mate did reach England for convalescence, though whether he was ever fit to return to the front I do not know.

The corporal rescued the gun and ordered us down the steps to safety. For two hours the bombardment went on, pounding the earth mercilessly above our heads. We were deep enough to be safe and I realised, as I had not fully done before, how impossible it would have been to hold the position without these underground galleries. The bombardment ceased as suddenly as it had begun. When we rushed out into the trench—with the prospects of an enemy raid in our minds—there was little, except the reek of high explosive, to show that anything had really happened. Enemy lights continued to sail serenely above the battlefield. The company's gun teams had suffered several casualties, including the lance-corporal in charge of the neighbouring post, who had been killed.

The following afternoon the platoon lined the trench to hurl smoke bombs at a prearranged signal into No-man's-land. As occupants of the sentry post we were not enthusiastic about this. In our vulnerable situation we preferred to let sleeping dogs lie. As the smoke from the bombs billowed up, our colleagues hustled helter-skelter down the stairway, pursued by stray whisps of their own devising. Nor were they a moment too soon, for the enemy, suspecting a surprise attack, at once dropped his barrage upon us. If the ruse had been designed to disclose his gun positions it seemed to have been successful.

During these hectic hours there was a good deal of discussion among us over the conduct of the war, a subject upon which each considered himself an authority! Looking to the past rather than the future, the topic on this occasion was the respective discomforts and dangers of the Salient and the Somme. I plumped decisively for the Somme, whose evils I knew I should never get out of my soul. The Salient, I conceded, might be more deadly, but here everything was better organised. These saps for instance, spelt safety. The rations came up regularly: there was even hot food and drink, a warm and dry place to sleep in at night. No, I would not have exchanged Hill 60 for Flers Switch. But the old hands were equally convinced, and I have no doubt we were not comparing like with like, for the 23rd Division had left the Somme before the weather broke. Moreover, they had served in well-organised units under officers who bothered about the welfare of their men and took their responsibilities seriously.

Our rations here were reasonably good. Hot stew and tea were conveyed along the trench from the cookhouse at the back of the hill in flat barrel-like containers with screw-down lids which were strapped over the orderly's shoulders. On one occasion the orderly—a somewhat feckless member of the company who was often assigned to this particular job to keep him out of harm's way—had failed to secure the lid properly. On his way back a shell had burst uncomfortably near the trench, causing him to bend low. His arrival at the platoon literally soaked with bully-beef stew would have been a matter for laughter had the liquid not been so precious. Bread was bulky to carry into the trenches and often short in consequence: equally the loaves, well-shaped cottage loaves when they left the army bakehouse, were apt to get battered and arrive in pieces with a veneer of sacking fibres. Corporal Goffee, true to his experience as an old campaigner, was expert in cutting a loaf into the maximum number of slices. He could extract a score or even more from a sound loaf and his skill was in demand for this menial office. Nor was he the man to stand on his dignity on such occasions, as most corporals would have done. We all knew him as one who had marched with the pukka soldiers on the frontiers of India, which to us was a place of myth and magic and, certainly to me, of glory, for I was born in an age when Englishmen were still proud of their heritage and not made shamefaced by the mere utterance of the word 'Empire'.

On that evening we were relieved of our front-line duties and ordered down into deep support, where we were to be employed on working parties. Deep down in the bowels of the earth, much lower than we had hitherto penetrated, we occupied a well-boarded chamber, double-decked and large enough to hold all the platoon. Here it was possible to obtain a more extensive, though no doubt still very partial, picture of the wonderful underground fortress by which the entire hill seemed to be honeycombed. The galleries were like the internal organs of some huge monster to which we humans, like mites within, gave life through our apparently haphazard activities. All the time there was the incessant chug-chugging of the machinery, and the movement of waters along the gutters which drained the passages. The sounds of war were far away above, although now and again a particularly heavy shell caused the galleries to reverberate. It was altogether an incredible place, the culmination of endless labours now on the point of fruition.

From the greater safety of that comfortable underground billet the outer world seemed even more frightful, if that were possible. That same night we were taken down the Railway Cutting and across to a dump masked by a low bank, where we were set to carrying ammunition, not an easy job under the best conditions. In the darkness and under bombardment, or the fear of bombardment, which caused us to hurry, the task taxed my strength to the limit. At the end of three hours, when it was time to withdraw, I was reduced to exhaustion and on the verge of tears, which I found extremely difficult to suppress.

The next morning, immediately after I had drawn my fried bacon, I was unfortunate enough to be detailed to assist the Australian Tunnelling Company, who had been carrying out mining operations towards the enemy positions for months on end, working day and night in six-hour shifts. This had been a war of wits. At times the Germans' counter-mining had brought the enemy so close to the saps that galleries had been blown. There had even been hand-to-hand fighting underground, and new galleries had had to be made, each side striving to get beneath the other. We had retained the ascendancy and a vast mine was now approaching completion. Immense quantities of ammonal had been buried and arrangements were already in hand for blowing the charge by electric ignition from behind the line. Our job on this particular morning was to help with the construction of sandbagged barriers to tamp the charge and prevent blow-back along the galleries.

We were conducted by the free-and-easy Australian sergeant through a wonderful labyrinth of passages until we reached an opening into a sort of calm cul-de-sac outside the hill, where the air was fresh and the light seemed brilliant after being so long below ground. A high and considerable breastwork of sandbags zigzagged away to our right. The ground beyond rose to a low ridge in the middle distance. There was nothing the least ominous about that desolate scene: nothing moved and there was unusually little noise. We were pleased to be enjoying the sweet spring air even in such a setting. The working party spread out round a bend in the breastwork, forming a human chain to transport bags from the farther edge, into the galleries, for use in the tamping operation.

As it happened I was the end man in the chain and was standing at the corner of a traverse where the breastwork turned abruptly leftwards and quickly petered out in the waste. We worked with a will, for the task was a light one and the fresh air filled us with new vigour. We were pleased, too, by the novelty of the work and the friendly attitude of the N.C.O. in charge. For once we quite forgot to grumble!

Indeed, there was poised just above the far horizon the black speck of an observation balloon, though our sense of direction gave us no indication whether it was friend or foe. It was a characteristic of the Salient that one could never be certain.

A little later an enemy battery began firing and shells burst along the ridge, not much more than a hundred yards away. Another salvo passed over and crashed on to the hill behind us. In the shelter of the breastwork we felt secure and it certainly did not occur to us that we might be the real target. We seemed to harbour a trustful feeling that we should not have been brought out there had there been any special danger. Against all experience and reason, we continued to have childlike trust in the omniscience of those in command, and on this occasion everything had so clearly been well planned that no question had entered our minds. By this time the work had progressed so well that the sergeant decided to lengthen the chain. Three of us moved round the corner.

Suddenly the battery began firing again, and there was something in the approaching scream that marked us as the target.

I cringed low as the first shell burst somewhere near the corner. Then we all began running like frightened rabbits back to the burrow, which now seemed so far away. As I turned the last bend a man a few yards ahead crashed to the ground. I recognised him as one of the youngsters of the recent draft and the very man who had just taken up the place at the corner I had vacated. Aided by the man just ahead, I attempted to lift our stricken comrade, but he was too stiff and heavy and we were now out there alone, some fifty yards or so from the sap entrance. A second salvo left the guns and terror took control of my senses. The next thing I knew was that I was leaning breathlessly against the timbers of the opening, panting and frightened. The rest of the party bunched undecidedly in the entrance. Shells were now lashing the breastwork but a little way from the opening which, however, was out of the line of fire. Here was safety; out there, but a few yards away, pain and sudden death. Our Australian N.C.O. decided to report back to his headquarters for instructions.

Corporal Bell of our company, a quietly-spoken Londoner and commercial clerk in civil life, now appeared on the scene, elbowing his way through the indecisive crowd. On learning what had happened, which was not an easy matter for we were all talking at once, he demanded why we had not brought the casualty in. Our assertion that he was dead did not satisfy the corporal. 'Come on, one of you men,' he said; 'we must bring him in.' No one budged. I felt ashamed, but had no intention of going out there again unless I was directly ordered. Why shouldn't someone else go?

Time seemed to stand still. The corporal lost patience: a last appeal and he started off alone. He doesn't know what it was like, I thought. Then something stirred to override my fears. He couldn't possibly be allowed to go alone. Against all reason I followed him. We raced along the breastwork. All was again quiet. We bent to raise the prostrate figure, but death had rendered the task of moving such a rigid corpse beyond our united strength, weakened no doubt by the stress and excitement of the moment. Shelling recommenced, scattering bags from the breastwork all around us. 'Run!' shouted Corporal Bell, and with my remaining energies I ran as I had never run before, as a tornado of bursts smashed down the breastwork under the shadow of which we had just been stooping. The enemy had really found his target and we two were lucky to survive.

Later on it was reported that the stretcher-bearers, who eventually retrieved the body, were of the opinion that the dead man had been killed immediately, for he had shrapnel in his brain and about the heart. Yet I knew that he had run a number of yards before he fell!

We were relieved to hear that the outside work had been abandoned and we completed our spell moving the accumulated bags along the galleries in trolleys. As the shift ended at 2 p.m. the Australians issued us with a tot of rum, so large compared with our normal issue that I dropped into a deep sleep as soon as I reached the dug-out.

When I awoke the chamber was abustle with the issuing of tea and agog with dire tidings. Rumours had been going about for some days that important moves were pending. But rumour was always active in this way and I doubt whether any of us in the rank-and-file had allowed it to sink in. After all, secrecy was still part of official policy. Thus we had not really associated ourselves personally with the events that were fast maturing, nor taken the normal amount of interest in the clear signs that literally screamed the truth at us. In any case, it was always someone else who was to do the job! Thus the news now broke upon us with a shock. On the day after the morrow a great attack was being launched in which our battalion would take a foremost part. Our company was to hold a forward trench in close support during the initial attack. It was perhaps something not to be assigned to the first waves, but memories of a similar situation near the Butte de Warlencourt on the Somme during the autumn of 1916 offered little personal reassurance.

CHAPTER II

CAPTURE OF MESSINES RIDGE

On the following day—6th June—the day before the battle for which such extensive preparation had been made, we were back in the Bund dug-outs. It was a fine afternoon and the shattered city seemed to be resting peacefully in the bright spring sunshine. Its hour of deliverance was at hand. Yet all was still quiet on the Western Front, or so it must have appeared to the enemy, looking, as I was looking, upon the scene from afar. The Germans were expecting something, as official reports now show, but just what and when they did not know.

In the near distance, under the shadow of the bank of the Bund, the scene had already taken on an appearance of hectic activity unusual at that time of day. In the little stream that trickled down the embankment from the lake many of us were washing, perhaps for the last time on this earth. Some, whose helmets lacked the regulation canvas cover, were daubing the metal curves with mud to prevent shine. Officers were trying on their ranker's tunics, which would render them less conspicuous to the enemy. Stretcher-bearers, runners and others, some newly pressed into specialist services for the attack, were sewing distinctive badges on to their sleeves. On the embankment above a drooping notice-board, relic of a more leisurely phase of warfare, forbade fishing with Mills bombs, a sport we were hardly likely to indulge in at that moment. Tea was served and the fortunates who had been chosen to go back to the transport lines as reinforcements were preparing their departure. Time hung heavily on our hands. We spoke little, each in his own way dwelling upon the morrow and all the dire possibilities that fate might hold. There were few jokes and none of the usual ill humour. We were comrades in adversity, knowing that, as far as we were personally concerned, the hour of decision had passed.

As the dusk began to fall the landscape towards the town

gradually took on a new aspect. It was like a transformation scene on a vast stage. Out of Ypres crawled numerous tractors hauling heavy guns to take up positions on the flats in front. At some points the guns were positioned literally wheel to wheel and little attempt, as far as I could see, was being made to hide or even protect them. The guns were followed by men: in small groups at first, and then in long files reaching out like menacing tentacles into the Salient. Lastly, seeming to throw caution to the winds, field guns came galloping along the roads, followed closely by their ammunition trains. Surely in all its previous vicissitudes the Salient had never witnessed such a furious activity as this!

The major noises of battle continued to be stilled, only the continuous murmur of moving men and vehicles welling up out of the dusk. The hours moved slowly and the evening seemed endless. I tried to doze, but could not. We were all subdued, concerned with our most intimate thoughts. I had but one dream, the hopeless dream that I might awake to find it all a dream.

* * *

At midnight we left the Bund along the duckboard track to Hill 60. Lying hard by the route near the end of the dug-outs I saw two shapes casually covered with a piece of sacking which left their blackened features exposed, an indication that they had long lain thus. In the hustle of preparing an attack the small services due to the dead had to take second place. In this hellish place there could be no peace, not even in death. Almost simultaneously the raucous blast of a strombus horn* came shatteringly from near at hand and the cry of 'gas' shuddered along the file. The enemy were strafing the area with gas shells, which whined over and struck the ground around us with their characteristically undecided thud, as though a burst had been intended but failed to materialise. The sickly smell of gas came to our nostrils as we hurriedly adjusted our respirators and stumbled through the danger zone. As always—or so it seemed to me—these shells inspired a fear that was out of all proportion to the damage done.

* A type used in military areas as a gas alarm.

Before reaching the comparative shelter of the communication trench, we crossed a track about which clung a strong reek of petrol as though a tank had recently passed this way. We were heartened by this thought and our tongues loosened to speculate what effect its appearance would have upon the Germans. As it happened, this was the only trace of a tank that I was to come across throughout the operations, but this fact signified little, for in such battles the participants rarely got more than a worm's-eye view of what was going on. Official records show that many tanks took part in the attack.*

It was about 2 a.m. when we reached the newly dug support trench, sited somewhere on the left flank of Hill 60. It proved to be little more than four and a half feet deep on the average and a very insecure position in which to withstand a bombardment. It seemed to me at once that this would do little more than attract the enemy fire, as had happened in my last battle on the Somme. No one liked the prospect before us: even Corporal Goffee, usually so phlegmatic, joined in the discussion which, of course, was just a waste of breath. We knew that our role had been assigned by the higher powers, whose planning could hardly take account of all our personal fears and reactions. There was also the unknown quantity of the great mine buried deep in the earth somewhere below us. Its probable effects were only hazily assessed. Anything might happen. We were instructed to be ready to leave the trench just before zero hour, in case the earth should close in upon us.

There was enough terror in those waiting hours to fill a lifetime. How our chatter affected Eldred I could not know, for he remained his quiet, thoughtful and uncomplaining self in a situation that he must at least have found bewildering.

The hours passed slowly. The night was clear and chill and unusually quiet. The guns on both sides remained silent. Ever and anon a lone light rose from the enemy line, spreading a lurid glare over the scene. Everywhere there was an illusion of stillness. Only those who had seen for themselves could have guessed at the tremendous activity and force now massing behind the low ridges of the Salient, an activity soon to burst across this stagnant scene. Such waiting was hardly bearable.

* See p. 77 below.

At last, as the first streaks of dawn began to steal across the heavens, whispered orders sent us to our positions, prone to the ground a few yards in front of the trench. These last minutes dragged away with agonising yet relentless slowness, as though death were in no hurry. Gradually the early greyness of a new day suffused the sky and began to light up the earth around us. I felt a tremor of fear run through my body as the deeper silence of the grave seemed to be enfolding the whole world.

With a sharp report a rocket began to mount into the daylit sky. A voice behind me cried, 'Now.' It was the hour, and that enemy light never burst upon the day. The ground began to rock. My body was carried up and down as though by the waves of the sea. In front the earth opened and a large black mass mounted on pillars of fire to the sky, where it seemed to remain suspended for some seconds while the awful red glow lit up the surrounding desolation. No sound came. My nerves had been keyed to sustain a noise from the mine so tremendous as to be unbearable. For a brief spell all was silent, as though we were so close that the sound itself had leapt over us like some immense wave. Almost simultaneously a line of men rose from the ground a short distance in front and advanced away towards the upheaval, their helmets silhouetted and bayonets glinting in the unearthly redness. I saw no more.

We hurled ourselves back across the still trembling earth into the trench. There was a tremendous roar and a tearing across the skies as the barrage commenced with unerring accuracy. It was as though a vast door had been flung open, and the silence died within the instant. The skies behind our lines were lit up by the flashes of many thousand guns, while above the booming din of the artillery rose the rasping rattle of the Vickers guns, pouring from their carefully prepared positions a continuous stream of lead into the enemy lines. Never before surely had there been such a shattering bombardment, and for a brief moment my sympathies went out to the unfortunate enemy caught in such a storm of death!

Such altruistic thoughts were immediately negated. Though taken by complete surprise, the enemy gunners were not slow in answering their SOS calls. Even as I fell towards the trench their shells were already bursting around. The gaping trench loomed up towards me and in my excitement I slipped upon the edge and lurched, head foremost, amidst a rain of loose earth. My steel helmet slipped off, and I was only able to drag clear my Lewis-gun ammunition buckets before a stream of humanity, struggling instinctively towards the deeper reaches of the trench, carried me before it. During the ensuing bombardment I could think of little else than my lost helmet. In some ways this may have been a good thing, though my state was pathetic. As in a dream my exposed head assumed exaggerated proportions in that mad situation.

The shells were lashing the ground in fury, literally fringing the trench, each piece of flying shrapnel seeming to be searching for my unprotected head. As I thrust it into the loose parapet, grains of earth matted my hair and trickled down inside the collar of my tunic. The rest of the section crouched around in the deeper and narrower corner of the trench where we had come to rest. Corporal Goffee sat doubled up in the corner, his knees almost to his chin. Except for an occasional blasphemy or a laconic 'The next one'll get us', he remained motionless. Eldred, next to me, leaned against the parapet, his eyes closed as though overwhelmed by it all, while a little farther along Hardcastle cried audibly. From right and left arose cries of pain, and already the stretcher-bearers, risking all in the course of duty, were pushing backwards and forwards to dress the wounded.

My own particular predicament remained uppermost in my mind. If only I could get a steel helmet! Crash! I grovelled even further into the muck as a cloud of acrid fume swept down into the trench. A runner scrambled past. Had he by chance seen a spare helmet? He merely shrugged his shoulders: he had much more important business to occupy his mind. The din continued, the earth throbbing rhythmically with the discharge of the guns. The air was charged with the smell of high explosive. Our lives seemed limited to the next explosion. Fortunately for us the enemy batteries were badly disorganised and their shooting consequently somewhat haphazard. Certainly our casualties were steadily mounting, but so far fortune had smiled upon the gun team.

In retrospect I am sure that the sheer magnitude of events at that point of time was diminished in my own mind to the mere consequences of losing a steel helmet. I felt like a crab without its shell, although, in fact, the protective capacity of a steel helmet in such circumstances was extremely limited. This was no doubt nature's way of shielding us from madness and, had I been aware, I should no doubt have discovered similar preoccupations in the minds of each of my companions.

Runners reported the success of the first advance with comparatively light casualties. After a lull our guns broke into renewed fury and it was clear that the attack was being further developed. The crack of rifles and rattle of machine-guns came back clearly through the din. This could be explained by the fact that we were near the left flank of the attack, where the thrust was not so deep as farther away to our right. This time casualties were much heavier. Once more the bombardment died down and obviously the time for consolidation had arrived. In the meantime, except for the occasional shell-burst, we were being left alone.

It must have been towards midday when orders came for us to move forward and we filed along the battered trench. Our wounded had already been carried away, but the whole area was in a chaotic state. I soon found the steel helmet for which I had been craving and which its erstwhile owner no longer needed. I felt safer at once and my horizon automatically widened. It was at this stage that I saw two of our runners sniping at German prisoners, who were trickling back in twos and threes across the broken ground in front. Both were normal, kindly fellows in ordinary times, loving fathers of families. Such incidents have been frequently quoted in the war literature as typical of both sides, but the particular incident was unusual in my experience, the aberration of individuals under incalculable stress.

The trench now began to lose itself in broken ground, the parapet becoming less and less well defined, affording less and less protection. Away in the distance I glimpsed a vista of trees. Certainly the attack had already changed our world out of all recognition! At this point we got hopelessly involved with a carrying party coming in the opposite direction. Curses were freely exchanged and the competence of our leaders volubly questioned. At this moment the Germans must have spotted us, for they began sniping with whizz-bangs. These swiftly moving miniature shells always put the wind up us more than anything else. They rushed at one with a scream, the noise of the discharge from the gun and the burst being almost simultaneous. There was practically no warning. We found the ground again with our stomachs.

Something had gone wrong. We were not wanted after all. Orders were passed along for us to turn back. Eldred, who had been just behind me, was now a step or so ahead. We had hardly moved in this reverse direction when, with another frightening screech, a shell hit the parapet while a second burst on the parados inside the trench between us. I was lifted bodily and enveloped in a suffocating cloud of yellow fumes. I felt wildly about my body with hands which seemed to belong to a different being, swayed on the side of the trench, and then took to my heels in terror. I saw dimly, but only half comprehendingly, a prostrate form on the trench bottom. I had completely lost my head. With teeth chattering I screamed 'Stretcher-bearers', saw shadowy forms moving ahead of me and somehow arrived back in the deeper part of the trench, where the company had again halted.

How long I remained half-conscious, I do not know. It was fortunate for me that we were under cover, with nothing for the moment expected of us. Probably my immediate companions were just as upset as I was, and not therefore predisposed to examine my conduct too closely. I was quite helpless. As comprehension gradually returned, voices seemed to be coming from far away. 'Your pal was badly hurt'. 'We thought you were, too.' Then I began to realise that it was Eldred lying there and that I had left him. My conscience took over the office of judge. Why had I left him? I should have known. Why hadn't I been hit also? The shell burst close enough. It must have blown all in his direction. Poor Eldred. Lucky devil. To be out of this. God, what a hell! A trench, a burrow, death. Burial comes sometimes just a little out of sequence.

Back in the old trench, there was nothing to do now but to wait—for the next order, or death, whichever came first. It all seemed immaterial. Little by little the outside world reimposed itself upon my consciousness. Little by little I came back to present reality. And as my mind cleared, even stronger became my inclination to envy my companion in his misfortune. To be out of this present, ever-present, eternally present misery, this stinking world of sticky, trickling earth ceilinged by a strip of threatening sky. Men crouched around. They told me that Eldred had been badly hit, but that he had been taken away quickly to the dressing-station. My conscience pricked me. I blamed myself bitterly for not having stayed with him. This was just as unreasonable as most of the ideas that had been streaming through my mind. I had lost all sense of volition, a thing that had never happened before and was never to happen again in that war. It had been the closest escape for me and it cannot be doubted that at that dire moment my good fortune exceeded all reasonable measure.

By this time the bombardment had died away. Bursts of machine-gun fire could still be heard occasionally, far away in the distance. The main advance had apparently ceased. Offensive action was now being concentrated upon individual points of resistance. The enemy, too, was able to take stock and it was now that our position appeared as most vulnerable. As it happened the Germans' observation from the Left Sector was unimpaired and we were a prominent target. His guns from that quarter were able to take us from the rear, and partly in enfilade. They now began to subject us to an unhurried, methodical and deadly bombardment. This was the last straw and it seemed that our nerves must break under the strain. Shrapnel whizzed and spattered into the trench. For me the earlier fears were transmuted into a terror that was hardly bearable. With every approaching scream, every cry for stretcher-bearers, I seemed to be torn apart. These were the worst moments of the whole battle, and yet my nerves did not give way. At length the enemy gunners were satisfied with their work and comparative peace settled over our corner of the battlefield. But more casualties had been added to our quota.

* * *

It was late in the afternoon when orders came for us to draw bombs from a trench store and proceed to Battle Wood as reinforcements. The fact that this was what we were there for did not render this move any the more welcome. The morning's events had knocked the stuffing out of us, even though our contribution to the battle so far had amounted to no more than the infantryman's role of standing like pawns on a board whose 'game' was both outside his range of vision and beyond his understanding. We halted at the store, waiting for others to draw their loads. In any case, the Lewis-gun team was already sufficiently burdened with the spare buckets of ammunition. As we dallied my eyes fell upon a dead soldier sprawled along the trench's edge. He was about my own age: his ashen, youthful face was twisted in pain and his unseeing eyes seemed to be questioning the skies. There were no signs of blood or mutilation. It was just a corpse. Yet amidst all the bloody sacrifice of the day that figure stands out still in my memory. His mother bore him that he might die just like that. I could not but wonder, gratefully and with selfish reflection, why it had been that unknown rather than myself.

We crossed the shell-torn Hill 60 and I looked about me with wonder. All the ground where our trench had run was pocked so closely with shell-holes that they touched and overlapped, disproving the widely held view that no two shells ever fell in the same place. It was here that enemy barrages had fallen constantly both before and during the battle. We worked our way along the top of the Railway Cutting and came upon the crater of the mine we had seen exploding, one of a whole series that had been detonated under the Messines Ridge that morning. What I had expected to see I had, of course, not clearly visualised—a jagged hole, perhaps, immense and heaped up with debris and fearful remains! The reality was quite unexpected—a large flat-bottomed depression, shaped like an immense frying-pan, clean and clear of debris except at the farther edge, where vestiges of an enemy trench showed through its sides. On the nearer lip, facing our lines, sprawled the immense figure of a German infantryman, a veritable giant of a man, still clutching his rifle. A murmur of approbation passed down the file, not, for once, for the death of an enemy but in admiration of a brave man. It may be that his story was unseen and has never been told, but it seems probable that he was out in an advanced post near our line when the mine went up behind him, and that he had been able to get back to the newly made crater and to begin at once to fire at the advancing line, one man against an army. The vision of his last moments can only be imagined.

As we continued our winding way across the waste towards Battle Wood, the vast battlefield widened before me, touched off here and there by black fountains of bursting shells which, in a leisurely manner, compared with what had gone before, were searching out targets among the moving groups of men now pursuing their several missions between the lines. I became vividly conscious of a new strangeness about it all. This was the typical battlefield that I had seen before, and yet not typical as part of a battlefield which, until that morning, the ordinary infantryman had had little opportunity of surveying; certainly not from a walking position. For many months past no human being had stood there in broad daylight and lived. The Salient, as so many had known it, was no more.* This was the first obvious result of the morning's operations. For once the first fruits of battle were plain to those taking part.

We crossed the enemy's erstwhile support trenches and halted thereabouts while runners went forward for further instructions. It seemed foolhardy to hang about in such an open situation without proper cover, but there was nothing else to be done, for orders had been issued that on no account was the enemy line to be occupied. His trenches were of a very different construction from ours, being revetted with brushwood which looked very flimsy to us compared with our own heavily sandbagged emplacements; in fact, neither type had come off very well in the recent shelling. Our sappers were already at work along the edge of the wood, which began a little way over to our right. They were probing the ground for concealed saps, or possibly mines, for it was known that the Germans had been active underground in the area.

While we waited it rained heavily, drenching us to the skin. By the time orders arrived for us to move forward the Germans, who had obviously decided that we were a worth-while target, began to shell the area with 5.9s† and to hunt us along the edge of the wood. Consequently we broke into scattered groups and most of the Mills bombs were dumped on the way. On the far

* See map, p. 10.

† Shell from a heavy howitzer gun of 15 cm. calibre.

edge of the wood, where the Comines railway crossed between the trees, there was a gap thinly held by a Yorkshire regiment, which we were being called upon to reinforce. The Germans still held a corner of the wood, where the exchange of rifle shots told us that skirmishing was taking place. The situation was obviously pretty fluid. But with our arrival the enemy must have decided to withdraw. With the coming of dusk, activity subsided.

By this time the company were scattered about the wood in shell-holes and any depression affording cover, awaiting the next move. Corporal Goffee and three other members of the team, including myself, had occupied a short shallow trench which seemed to provide a suitable gun position. We set about deepening it with our entrenching tools. It was getting dark rapidly when a red light went up among the trees in front, spreading its warning glow eerily through the branches. Once more we were bombarded and now we prepared for the counter-attack which appeared to be developing. Once more we bent double in our hiding-places, and once more cries for stretcher-bearers were raised in tones of anguish. Once more the storm subsided: the threat had failed to develop.

Yet the outlook was hardly a hopeful one. We were very cold from the soaking, and hunger was beginning to get the upper hand. Our corporal hazarded the opinion that we should stand little chance if the Germans attacked, but set us to cleaning our arms in the darkness, as a routine precaution. We had the usual feeling after a battle that we had been abandoned. We knew that there were no supports immediately behind us, that we were a very thin shield between the enemy and the conquered territory. Our officers also seemed to lack assurance and to be little better informed than we were. They realigned us across the corner of the wood and we gathered that at dawn we were to make a local assault to straighten the line.

Terror and the elements failed to keep sleep at bay. The leaf-mould under the trees made a comfortable couch on which to wear off some of the accumulated fatigue of the preceding twenty-four hours. How long I slept I cannot say. I became conscious of voices close at hand saying, 'Thank God, the attack is off.' I had already begun to move purposefully, to hide the guilt of having slept, before the full meaning of these words struck home. Things like that did happen in dreams, I thought, as I rose up mechanically to follow the moving figures, glad that no one had noticed I had been sleeping.

Now all was abustle and there was no time to be lost. The news was true. We were to dig in without delay and to get below ground before daybreak, which could not be far off. With the few picks and shovels that had been salvaged we worked in shifts. Fortunately the ground was not hard and progress was rapid. From the chatter of my companions I gathered that the night had not passed quite so quietly as I had thought. There had been snipings and incidents. Paddy, the butt of so many jokes, had attempted to light a cigarette behind a tree-trunk. A companion spotting his intention had knocked him down, where he lay shouting: 'Sure, oim hit, oim hit!' Paddy's leg was now being pulled unmercifully among the working groups, but, as usual, he took all the badinage in good part.

Our rough-and-ready ditch got steadily deeper. The dawn was near at hand. Fritz began shelling the wood again. Most of the shells fell wide, but a salvo of whizz-bangs bursting near the new trench wounded a man a few paces away. He was one of the company's original members. His wound was serious and he had to be borne away.

It was decided now that, to evade discovery, we should take cover in the trench and complete it as best we could with our entrenching tools. We were down between four and five feet, a narrow slit in the ground, leaving little scope for us to turn about, but on the other hand affording the maximum cover in the circumstances. I scooped out a seat for myself on the bottom. Our line ran through a little glade near the edge of the wood. On our left the trench linked up with some German dug-outs. A low broken wall cut diagonally across our right flank, leaving a very limited field of fire for the gun. The trench did not seem at the time to be very well sited. Just in front there was a grave with a massive black cross encircled by a wreath of imitation ivy. During our stay we debated seriously and at length the origins of that grave, whose occupant must have felt considerably honoured by so much posthumous consideration! I do not recollect that we came to any final conclusion. It seemed to have a look of permanence and could well have belonged to a well-to-do Flemish person in a peacetime graveyard. There were flowers amidst the confusion, as though this had recently been a garden. All the trees of the wood were shattered at the top and many cast down in confusion, but unlike so many shattered woods in the battle line this one was still clothed with shoots and young leaves to show the colour of the season. Behind us the trees receded into the distance, where they eventually coalesced into one wall of silent trunks. Over to our right there was little visibility, but to the left the wood quickly ended at a broad waste of open shell-torn ground, so different from where we were. The contrast made it look a little unreal, like the drop-scene on a stage. It was from this flank that enemy observation was to be feared, for the left sector must have still curved back in that direction, where the advance had been minimal.

The next two days in our narrow trench gave us—bearing in mind the magnitude of the battle—little to grumble at. In fact, we did grumble, bitterly. To be cooped up together in such a situation for forty-eight hours may not sound much—and it wasn't much compared with other experiences at that time—but it was no joke. We had little to eat or drink at the outset and it was cold at night: we were packed together; there were calls of nature to be met, and all that.

During the first day the German artillery, now pulled back and dug into new positions, became more and more active. Gradually the wood came under almost continual bombardment as a likely cover for any further moves we might have in mind. Fortunately much of this shelling was blind or directed mainly at the abandoned German dug-outs, which were presumably the only map references the gunners had. As it happened, these had not all been left unoccupied and, much against advice, some had sought amidst their shelter such comfort as the rest of us could not hope for in the open trench. A heavy shell fell squarely on top of one dug-out, hitting every one of its thirteen occupants, mostly original members of the company. The majority were killed outright, while the wounded were so bad that none was expected to survive. This was a great blow, leading, of course, to the evacuation of all the dug-outs. We had one peculiar casualty to a company character. Shells were bursting out in front, keeping our heads well down, when something big came hurtling through the air with a sort of droning howl and landed with a resounding flop on its target. We had screwed ourselves into the wierdest attitudes, expecting some new type of missile. It was the flat back of a small shell and our Paddy was the victim. It had landed fair and square upon his box respirator, tied in the alert position across his chest. This it flattened, but, despite the force of the impact, Paddy was fortunate enough to get off with a severe bruising and dispatch to the dressing-station. His respirator had undoubtedly saved his life, but in a manner for which it was not designed!

Fortunately, on the 8th June, the first night following the attack, our carrying party brought up rations, water and rum without mishap and the pangs of hunger and thirst were assuaged. The night was very cold and the damp began to eat into our bones. We were getting on each other's nerves, feeling murder at the least provocation. With the approach of dawn we waited in a state of tension, expecting a counter-attack, which did not materialise. The trench bottom was getting into a state from human waste, our restricted movement during daylight making it impossible to get out.

That second morning was bright, with the spring sunshine gilding the surviving foliage, while a gentle breeze brought a happy rustle through the blasted wood. There were other sounds throughout that day: whining shells in our rear, spreading further destruction in nature's domain. One hit a tree close to the ground, toppling it towards our trench, which it just missed. The shells had a peculiar drone, coming from behind. At the time we thought they were from our own guns firing short, and we were very critical of the gunners. This sort of thing often happened in battle, especially when the new positions were not clearly defined, but on this particular occasion an alternative explanation was that the firing was by enemy artillery behind the Left Sector.

My statement about the total evacuation of the German dugouts was not quite true. The company's stretcher-bearer, Private Bell—known lovingly as Kidder Delicate on account of his portly robust appearance—having decided that comfort came before safety, slept in one of them on the second night. He was a fat, lazy and easy-going person in normal times, who became a fearless, self-sacrificing hero when there was any succouring to be done. His good temper, carried almost to the limits of non-involvement, made him a favourite in the company, and he could almost get away with murder. After the recent disaster, no one else would have dared to put his nose inside these dug-outs, but Bell must have been entirely without nerves —or imagination—and his occupancy of the dug-out against orders was typical of him. He richly deserved his subsequent decoration with the Military Medal.

On the night of the 9th our relief came in unheralded. There was but a bare strip of trench to be handed over, a ditch in a poor hygienic state, and nothing to delay our departure. The enemy artillery was dropping a stiff barrage on the wood, being pretty sure of catching such movements as this in progress. We were fortunate in being able to take a route out of the wood along the cutting to our objective behind the now deserted Hill 60. Tired, hungry and frightened, this proved a nightmare journey, every step of which, however, was spurred by the thought that it was one step nearer to safety and rest. The one overriding idea that kept running through my mind was of the pity it would be to get killed after coming through so much! I do not recollect that, in fact, we had any casualties on this occasion. At last the welcome and known shelter of the Bund dug-outs took us into its possession and we sank into that deep relaxing sleep that escape from danger induces.

The next morning all was bright and it was a joy to be alive, until one remembered missing friends. The company had suffered more than forty casualties. The men who had been held back as reinforcements came up to rejoin us and were received with the patronising air of men who have experienced something others have evaded. A day or two before we had envied them their good fortune: now we were inclined to regard them with feelings akin to pity. Such is the way of the world.

First reports were already placing the recent battle as a great victory and we were feeling pride at having taken part. On our front, where the advance tapered off into the old line to the north, its depth had been at its least, but over to the right the enemy's positions had been deeply penetrated and the whole of the Messines Ridge, with its splendid vantage-points, had fallen into our hands. On the right flank the Australians and New Zealanders had been involved in heavy fighting, but generally the enemy had been surprised and literally overwhelmed by the massiveness of the blow we had struck.*

Our colleagues told us that they had all assembled at points of vantage in the early hours of the morning of 7th June—as indeed had the brass-hats in droves—to see the mines go up. The detonation of the nineteen massive charges all along the ridge had been a magnificent and awe-inspiring sight. We on the spot had been involved in only one of the explosions and then too close to see the incident in perspective, but from the rear the whole line right across the sky seemed to be involved. The flashes were actually seen in Kent and many people on the other side of the Channel had heard distinctly the great roar as the battle opened up.

When we left the Bund and on the following day went into bivouacs in the reserve areas, the battle was still not quite over. In the line we had been expecting and dreading the enemy's counter-attack. Now the artillery on both sides was rather more active than usual. Enemy shells were continually bursting in the camp area, sometimes near the tents, causing us to run for shelter. On the night of 11th June the whole area was in a turmoil, our low-pitched bivouacs being lit up almost continuously by our gunfire and enemy shell-bursts, although I was still too tired to be much disturbed by this particular occurrence. At the time we thought the enemy attack was at last taking place and we were congratulating ourselves at having got clear in time. It seems, however, that the situation was rather different. There had already been local counter-attacks, but none on our sector. The enemy was too badly shaken to stage a major come-back. Possibly the night's uproar was due to some straightening-up process that was taking place farther along the front. The Battle of Messines was over and there were apparently no plans for immediate exploitation of our gains. That these gains had been sufficient completely to change the situation in the Salient our experience was quickly to show.

* See Historical Note on p. 76.

The battle's evil to both sides in human sorrow was heavy enough to dim any joy in its success. For myself I did not realise straight away the extent of my personal loss. I had heard of the severity of Eldred's wounds, but only slowly had brought myself to fear the worst. Now I learned from Company Office on the morning of our arrival in camp that he was dead. He had been taken back to the advanced dressing-station at Railway Dug-outs, where he died of wounds. I heard that he had been buried in the cemetery there, but after the war careful inquiries failed to find his grave, hardly a matter for surprise when one remembered how that evil-smelling place was always being churned up by enemy action.

I felt this loss very much, comparing it with the death of Jimmy Downs on the Somme. Even in the short period of our acquaintanceship Harold and I had become very close friends. Now I was faced with the unwelcome duty of writing to his home, a duty I had no intention of shirking on this occasion. Thus I sat down and wrote my unwelcome note in halting self-conscious English to the two dear middle-aged publicans in Peckham who were his parents and who—as I could not have anticipated at the time—I was one day to meet. No doubt, by practically the same post they would have received a more polished, but semi-officially worded, letter bearing the same tidings, from Second-Lieutenant Edwards, our platoon commander, whose duty it was to write letters of condolence on such occasions.

After the war I did meet Harold's parents, quiet, kindly God-fearing citizens who remained friendly with me until they died some time in the 'thirties. It seems to me that there can be few greater sacrifices in life than that of parents who lose a son who has reached manhood, particularly when it happens through the senseless chance of war. At that time few of us thought that way, and I doubt whether those good souls ever considered their sacrifice as fruitless and evil. They mentioned the small pathetic things that had been sent home, and could not understand why a gold wedding ring which Harold had worn was not included. I could guess what had happened, for robbery of the dead was but an incident of war not considered a crime—as, of course, it was. The worthless sentimental things were carefully put aside to be sent home, but anything of market value was likely to disappear before any official inventory had been made, if ever it was made. The 'finder' would argue that if he did not take it the next would, a natural utilitarian morality in the shadow of death.

THE BATTLE OF MESSINES, 7TH JUNE 1917

A plan for a major offensive in Flanders, prepared early in 1916, had been progressively modified under the pressure of serious developments, first at Verdun and later on the Somme, until only a limited attack upon the Messines Ridge, fixed for 15th July of the same year, remained, and this, too, had to be dropped or, rather, as things were to work out, placed in cold storage.

Along this particular sector of the front, where the ground was suitable, a deep mining offensive had been going on underground between Briton and German since 1915. Obviously the preparation of a number of immense mines, with which it was designed to reduce the might of this great defensive position, was not a matter for improvisation. Thus arrangements for the attack were already well advanced when it was decided early in 1917 to go ahead with the offensive. The new plan, taking into account the lessons of the past, particularly of the Battle of the Somme of the previous year and the more recent Battle of Arras, was completed by 3rd April.

The actual attack, due to be launched on 7th June, was preceded, from 21st May, by a systematic bombardment of accumulating intensity. This was greatly assisted by a period of fine weather which provided the British gunners with first-rate observation. The artillery paid special attention to the German network of pillboxes, a special feature of the Ypres front, which had been spotted by British observers and had the disadvantage from the defence's standpoint of showing up clearly—as soon as the preliminary shooting had cleared away the loose covering soil—the concrete in its pristine whiteness. Nevertheless these effective strong-points had to receive a direct hit to put them out of action, as the attackers were to discover to their cost.

The assault began at 3.10 a.m. on the appointed day along the entire length of the strongly fortified Messines Ridge, extending some ten miles from the small hamlet of St. Yves near Ploegsteert Wood, northwards to Mount Sorrel just beyond Hill 60. The aim was to remove the considerable enemy bulge into the British positions south of Ypres and to abolish the dangerous salient by which that key city had so long been menaced. The thrust involved a penetration of one to two miles into the German positions, tapering away to the north.

This was considered quite a considerable advance under the existing conditions of trench warfare. Along this front all the nineteen massive mines were successfully exploded as planned, throwing the enemy defences into confusion as the advance began.

*The mine under Hill 60 mentioned in the text was the most northerly of the nineteen, but there was a second nearby on the other side of the Railway Cutting. Although by no means the largest of these mines, this was a considerable detonation, containing a charge of some 53,500 lb. of high explosive, mainly ammonal. The other mine just mentioned (of which the present author was not at the time aware, although it was comparatively near) had a charge of 70,000 lb.**

Over one hundred battalions of infantry, numbering some 80,000 men, took part in the attack. These forces, belonging to General Plumer's Second Army, were deployed from right to left of the line of attack in the following order: on the right flank II ANZAC Corps, comprising the 3rd Australian Division, the New Zealand Division and the 25th Division; in the centre IX Corps, comprising the 36th (Ulster) Division, the 16th (South Irish) Division and the 19th (Western) Division; and on the left X Corps, comprising the 41st Division, the 47th (London) Division, with the 23rd Division on the flank. Seventy-two tanks of an improved type were assigned to the operation, specifically to assist the infantry in capturing the numerous strong-points. This was not a very large armoured force even at that time. (It is not surprising that on such a long battle-front the author should have come no nearer to meeting a tank than smelling its petrol trail on the way into the line, and this probably belonged to one of the older-type vehicles which, according to the Official History, *had been stripped of their armaments to facilitate the transport of supplies for the battle).*

By 9 a.m. the first objectives had been attained and the summit of the Ridge was in British hands. Casualties so far had been unusually light, but this fact in itself caused congestion in the new front line and failure to clear it undoubtedly added to the high proportion of casualties suffered later. The immediate counter-attack expected from the enemy did not develop, while on the British side an undue amount of time seems to have been spent in regrouping.

* History of the Great War: Military Operations France and Belgium 1917, Volume II (H.M.S.O. 1948). To be referred to in the text as *Official History*.

It was not until early afternoon that the German counter-assault began to develop, only to be frustrated by heavy artillery, machine-gun and rifle-fire before it could reach the advanced positions. The British advance to the final objectives was launched shortly after and this also was successful. Casualties were much heavier, the brunt falling upon the Australians in the centre in face of powerful resistance from the numerous German pillboxes.

Subsequent local British attacks were made on the 10th and 11th June, but these were relatively minor operations which hardly detract from the claim that the Battle of Messines was the most outstanding one-day success of the whole war.

Total British casualties amounted to 24,562, while the German figure was stated as 23,000, including 10,000 taken prisoner, but for various reasons these figures are not comparable.

On the contribution made by the author's division the Official History *confines its remarks laconically to:*

> *The 23rd Division, on the left, had heavy casualties in its efforts to clear Battle Wood, and its position on the northern flank was only consolidated after a long struggle. . . . The 11th Sherwood Foresters, on the extreme left, had some hard fighting to establish positions astride the maze of German trenches east of Mount Sorrel, and one part of its objective was not gained till late in the evening.*

The same authority sums up the entire battle as:

> *A great victory had been won by General Plumer's Second Army, and with a swift completeness beyond that of any previous major operation of the British Armies in France and Flanders. The capture of the Vimy Ridge, a lesser operation which the Second Army had taken as a model, alone bears comparison. After two long years of patient endurance, the ambition to remove the Germans from the dominating southern face of the Ypres Salient had been realised and the aim of months of intensive labour and preparation was achieved.*

A German authority, General von Kuhl, commenting on the failure of the German command to carry out a preliminary withdrawal that had at the time been recommended, states that 'The German army would thereby have been spared one of the worst tragedies of the War' (quoted from his 'Der Weltkrieg, 1914–1918').

CHAPTER III

SUMMER SKIRMISHING

It was a great relief to find ourselves away from the line in the reserve area, but we were in canvas bivouacs and our situation was hardly restful. Occasionally an enemy shell, replying anaemically to our active artillery, screamed down into a neighbouring field, narrowly missing a hut or a group of tents. The Armourer-Sergeant inspected our rifles, and we wondered not entirely unvocally, about his cushy job away from the line. We were taken to Poperinghe to enjoy an ever-welcome bath, and we paraded for pay. As a single man with no deduction I was well satisfied with twenty francs, but the married, and all those who had heavily drawn on their resources for one reason or another, received only ten francs, and there was much grumbling.

As already mentioned, on the night of 11th/12th June the ground shook with the discharge of guns, while the flashing batteries, glimmering through the chinks of the bivouac, did their utmost to keep us awake; fruitlessly as far as I was concerned, for I was still very weary. The following morning we were told that our move into reserve for reorganization had been postponed and a tremor of fear passed down the lines. Thus we waited throughout a sweltering June day with the sun for once doing everything in its power to cancel out the spoiling effects of war.

Then in the middle of the following night orders arrived for our move to the rear of the battle zone and we rose in the cool dawn to the light of storm lanterns, for once not grumbling at the inconsiderateness of the authorities. Our previous fatigue vanished as if by magic. In good spirits we were marching away into the clean tidy countryside that looked to us very like heaven. Two hours had passed and it was still early, the sun only just beginning to shine down upon us. We were away from all military works with a prospect of neat fields, and here and there an occasional cottage, spread out before us. It was not difficult, even for the least musical, to sing:

> Oh, landlord, have you a good red wine, *parlez-vous*
> Fit for the soldiers in the line, *parlez vous* . . .
> Oh, landlord, have you a daughter fair, *parlez-vous*
> With bonny blue eyes and golden hair, *parlez vous* . . .

and so on *ad lib*, with much libidinous detail.

In front, still some distance away, an abrupt green hill literally shoots up from the flat, so out of tune with the rest of the landscape as to look as though it had been put there as an afterthought. It is the Mont des Cats, capped with a famous Trappist monastery whose servants are sworn to silence. The Mont is but one of a series of such miniature mountains rising sheer out of the plain to heights that are modest enough but exaggerated by the sudden contrast. Nearer the line its counterpart was Mount Kemmel, where there had been much fighting, while farther back there was the hill at Cassel.

By now there is more than a note of fatigue in the singing which only the salacious reflection upon the daughter's white limbs manages to keep at bay. Towards the end of our third hour we are halting at the foot of the Mont with the buildings of the silent monks standing clearly against the sky well above us, accompanied by a massive roadside crucifix and an old-world windmill. Emulating the legions of Rome, we are set to march over the knob instead of finding an easier route round. Now the gaiety is succeeded by indignation and curses spontaneously replace previous benedictions. In front our colonel, saturnine and unsmiling, albeit a fine figure of a man, rides on majestically, his well-groomed horse finding little impediment in the steep ascent. Upwards we march with no prospect of another halt before the regulation time. There is a certain lagging. 'Get up there!' shouts a sergeant, as a man lurches from the ranks. 'Come off that bloody horse,' murmurs a man in the next file, adding 'you black bastard'. But the column moves steadily forward, the lesser failings and protests of individuals being masked by the ruthless impetus of the machine. At last the hill is topped and we sink at the roadside for our well-earned rest. Below us the country spreads all around like some immense patch-work quilt, of the type many of us have in our homes, in half a dozen different shades of green, while along the horizon in our rear a line of ever-watching observation balloons marks the boundary between war and peace. Though I can look back with pleasure upon the prospect from that small summit I doubt whether the picture at the time gave me much joy. One effect of the war was to stultify any aesthetic feelings.

It was indeed a relief when we took off our packs amidst the bell tents by the diminutive hamlet of Le Thieushouk, about three kilometres from the foot of the Mont. Here amidst green fields, with but one or two village shops among the few farm buildings, it seemed to me that our days could be more than bearable. That evening, alone in more senses than one, I walked along the quiet country road to the neighbouring village of Fletre and felt myself a human being once again, able, if only for a few hours, to decide whither my legs should carry me.

We spent the next fortnight in this quiet rural setting. The parade ground, sited between the tents and the road, was fringed by trees under which it was pleasant to sit in the evenings, reading and writing letters home. There were all the usual inspections, including examination of our feet, to which a good deal of attention was given. Mine were standing up well, showing no traces of the previous autumn's damage.

One day we marched to the Brigade Baths which had been set up in a small village a kilometre or so beyond Fletre. As welcome as the bath—at least to those of us who still had money to spend—was the well-stocked canteen somewhat incongruously installed under the same roof. There was a small battalion canteen in a shanty at the entrance to our own camp, but it was usually sold out. On another occasion we were ordered to take all blankets and spare clothing to the army fumigator which had been set up temporarily in the village. This was a Heath Robinson kind of contraption, consisting mainly of a large barrel-shaped thing into which steam was pumped under pressure. The object was to kill our resident lice, but the effect, we were soon to be convinced—apart from making everything bedraggled and tarnishing the buttons—was to incubate a new generation of lice from the eggs with which the seams of our clothing were always prolifically sown. Within a matter of hours we became as itchy as ever. On reaching the chugging monster we had to take off our tunic and trousers and to wait around in our greatcoats while the machine did its worst. Dressed thus in our underclothing amidst the inhabited buildings of that little place we felt very much at a disadvantage, pulling our coats around us and watching fearfully lest some of the natives should stroll over to see what was going on. The unavoidable intimacies of army life had apparently not killed the natural modesty in which most of us had been brought up.

There were some incidents to break the gentle monotony of our parades. On the day following our arrival I remember how the peace of the surrounding lanes had been broken by the martial music of many bands, as detachments of the 47th London Division marched through to their rest area farther back. We lined the road to give them an encouraging cheer and, from the smallness of the marching groups, it was evident how sadly depleted they were. They had been with us in the Messines attack.

Twice we were visited by V.I.P.s Two days after our arrival the advent of the divisional general was forecast. From the earliest hour the camp was in a ferment, the sergeant-major, normally a quiet, businesslike person, being in a severe state of nerves, and we suffered accordingly. The battalion paraded and waited. General Babbington arrived at last, but immediately his informal manner convinced the rank and file that he was 'a decent old bird'. Much to the apparent dissatisfaction of the upper ranks, he dispensed with the usual evolutions and told us to sit down on the grass while he talked. This very unmilitary approach was well calculated to please the troops. After congratulating the battalion on its contribution to the recent operations and reading Sir Douglas Haig's order of the day, the general came round to chat with individuals here and there. It happened that he asked one of the company orderlies whether he had enjoyed the chewing-gum sent up during the recent battle. Everyone beamed as the general received an affirmatory answer, although most of us were far from clear as to what he was talking about. It happened that his next inquiry was addressed to Private Berry, whom I've already mentioned. Berry, a Kitchener's recruit who had been wounded at Gallipoli, was a man of independent spirit, and not having had any chewing-gum, he said so. How was this? The officers glared; explanations were mumbled. In reply to the general's further inquiries others, now taking courage, confirmed that no chewing-gum had reached the trenches. The general was very angry. He walked away in close conclave with the senior officers, whose obvious discomfiture was probably more comforting than the missing Wrigleys would have been to most of us.* Heartened by the general's solicitude, we left the parade ground in a much better mood than we had entered it.

The second important visit, which took place towards the end of our fortnight, was from no less a person than our army commander, General Plumer himself. He was a short, venerable-looking man, remarkably spruce for his age and keen in appearance, the type not inclined to overlook any sort of slackness on the part of the leaders. He had a great reputation among the troops, whom he always treated with consideration. His great reputation as a soldier was to be enhanced as the war proceeded and to survive its ending, as many did not. We were all delighted that afternoon to see our battalion leaders eclipsed by a much greater personality and power and being decisively put in their place, as they were so much in the habit of putting us in ours.

Then there was, one afternoon, a storm in a teacup which pointedly demonstrated that it was not authority but its misuse that made us savage. Our company commander, Captain West, had dismissed us to our tents a short while ahead of the scheduled time, for it was the custom for battalion orders to lay down a strict programme for our day's parades. It happened that the adjutant arrived on the scene at that moment. He made a great fuss and ordered a resumption of the parade. We were genuinely sorry for our immediate leaders and did our best to share the humiliation being suffered on our behalf. Captain West, quiet and gentlemanly, eschewing the army habit of hard swearing and never, in fact, raising his voice in anger, was universally liked and respected. We knew him to be brave and followed him with confidence. There was never the least hint of insubordination under his command. The Adjutant's performance on this

* This was the only occasion in my experience of such an issue to the troops.

occasion—however much he himself may have been the victim of circumstance—was a poor example in public relations.

I was already well settled in with my section, accepted as an old hand, and as a Lewis gunner I was fortunate most of the time to attend our own specialist parades, during which I was adding to my knowledge of the mechanics and handling of the gun. The gap left by Eldred's death was not to be easily filled, all my team-mates already having their own pattern of interrelationships, but the general comradeship left me with no acute feelings of loneliness. Indeed, in the gregarious life of the army the few moments one was able to snatch to oneself were precious to a youth of my type. I received much reading matter from home and the battalion's post was dependable and regular in its deliveries, another great contrast with my previous experience. Among the papers sent out by my mother was the green *Weekly Westminster*, which provided such a balanced view of the great events as they were taking place. The official information services were poor and it was only through one's budget from home that one could keep abreast with the shattering events in which we were so closely involved. In fact, my ever-flowing stream of newspapers, magazines and novels—much greater than that of any other member of the ranks—soon gained me a reputation and some popularity as an inexhaustible source of reading matter, and everything I passed on was eagerly devoured by other members of the platoon, including particularly the lead-swinging Irish Old Soldier whom I have already mentioned. He hated the authorities and was far from popular, except among a small circle of cronies, but he was never other than courteous and reasonable with me. I imagine his general attitude was attributable to his unreasoned resentment at the revolutionary upheaval which the war had administered to the habits of a lifetime. His expectations had been shattered. Hitherto he had avoided taking responsibility; now he found himself ordered about by every Tom, Dick and Harry and, as we said at the time, he was 'fed up to the back teeth'. He spoke with pride of the regiment's peacetime library, which he had explored thoroughly. I soon discovered that under his rough exterior he was the most widely read among my companions, although that is not perhaps saying very much.

There was another character whom I remember very well—

Peterson, the company bully—and this recollection is no doubt sharpened by the fact that he both disgusted and frightened me. He was a ship's painter in civil life, a burly, blustering type with a menacing expression that seemed to constitute a normal feature in his physiognamy. His strong card was his willingness to undertake the job of mess orderly, which was always unpopular, and thus to take a hand in serving the meals. His technique was to serve his cronies a little more liberally than the rest of us and, as supplies were rarely generous, this created widespread annoyance. He exercised his favouritism with a certain amount of discretion and was fiercely threatening at the least criticism. This was usually sufficient to quell any incipient opposition. The first time I was personally involved in an incident of this sort I was sufficiently annoyed to stand my ground, four square, albeit with quaking heart within, for I was no boxer and he was a most formidable-looking brute. Within my knowledge his actual pugilistic skill had not been demonstrated and it was to be a long time before it was. For the moment at least my rabbit courage served its purpose and, looking back, I think he must have put me on a sort of neutral list of those who were not prepared to play his particular game, for I rarely had further trouble with him, though I was often extremely annoyed on others' behalf.

Despite the almost inexhaustible flow of reading matter from home, additions to my store were always welcome. The few local shops sometimes displayed English paper-back magazines in the larger format of that time, which were priced at 6*d*., but usually sold at 4½*d*. at home. These were quickly snapped up, irrespective of title. The sentimental romances of such writers as Charles Garvice and Elinor Glyn were very popular. I remember one evening finding my way to Caestre, a village about three kilometres distant, where there had been established a well-equipped Church Army hut. There I discovered a small village shop kept by a friendly Frenchwoman from whom I purchased a number of English novels. She was older than I, of course, with all the traditional fascination of the Frenchwoman, and seemed inclined to hold me in conversation. My French was as halting as her English, but a native prudishness almost overwhelmed me with shyness and I saw gaping before me—quite unwarrantably no doubt—the most awful temptations. I beat a hasty and, I fear, in retrospect, a most unchivalrous retreat.

As I walked back, still flustered by my unsatisfying encounter, my imagination surveyed in vivid terms the possible delights and almost certain dangers that could have lurked behind that shop counter. I even wondered whether the books themselves might be just a blind. Rumours of goings-on in the countryside houses often came to one's ears, but I do not recollect that at that particular time sex was a foremost preoccupation of my companions. Many went only in search of an estaminet and sampled the local wine, which brought them back to camp in merry mood, except on pay night, when the more heavy drinking led to ructions.

Despite the pervading quiet of that pleasant countryside we were not altogether beyond the searching tentacles of the battle. As we sat by our tents in the sunshine we could observe the hedge of balloons along the horizon to the north. From time to time enemy planes made feints at the ungainly, vulnerable targets, causing their defenceless occupants to bale out hastily. We could see their shining parachutes far away, as they floated unhurriedly to the ground. The attacker, daring the anti-aircraft fire which had to avoid the balloons, swooped down and, using some type of igniting missile, brought down a number of them in flames. Such attacks were understandable, for these balloons helped us to cancel out the advantage the Germans had in occupying the higher ground on this front. At night there was increasing activity in the air behind our lines, as bombs were dropped on neighbouring villages: we felt reasonably secure in our flimsy camp, which was well camouflaged amidst the green fields. Later on the immunity of the back areas was to be sadly shattered and our troops were to find their rests in the rear much less restful.

If these reminders of actual war were to reinforce our pleasure at being for a while away from it all, our minds were menaced by the ever-present fear of the day that would herald our return to the line. Rumour, feeding on the absence of local news, was ever active, sowing doubts and disquiet in our minds. The authorities could not have been aware of the insidious nature of this attack on our morale, and did not realise therefore how worth while it would have been to organise an active news service to keep us in the picture. It is possible that our confusion of mind was accepted as desirable. If so, I am sure the authorities were absolutely wrong in this.

On the last day of June we regretfully left our quiet haven and took the road once again to 'oonoesware'. It rained unremittingly and we were soon slopping along like depressed, drowning rats. The stew which was served by the field kitchen at the roadside was hardly distinguishable from the rain itself, although through no fault of the cooks, whose strenuous efforts to keep the fires going were insufficiently appreciated at the best of times. That night we found shelter in a camp near the little village of Ochtezeele, and the proximity of war reinforced the morning's soaking further in depressing our spirits.

These feelings were artificially relieved on the second day of our return to the area of the camps by a pay parade, which that evening was celebrated in a local canteen well stocked with beer. The camp lines rang to the strains of 'Blaydon Races', a well-known Northumbrian song, very popular on such occasions. But the festivities did not stop at singing. There was a brawl, a number of the company, filled with Dutch courage, making a dead set at the Old Soldier. In the mêlée the combatants sprawled over the guy-ropes and many blows fell upon the wrong man. Then a bayonet was drawn and things began to look ugly. Fortunately the Old Soldier, more than a match for any of his opponents singly, now had the sense to make himself scarce. The rumpus subsided as the neutralists ostentatiously dissociated themselves from either faction.

A large draft from home had now joined us to fill the gaps left by the recent battle. They were all new to active service and had much to learn, a mixed group, coming from all parts of Britain. Among those whom I was to come to know very well were Tom Ireland, tram conductor from Bradford, old to us in his forties, with whom I was to maintain friendly correspondence right up to the eve of the Second World War, and Isaac Doniger, from Leeds, a kindly generous Jew whose friendship I treasured until his death in 1965. There was also Canelle,* a well-educated Second Division Clerk in the Civil Service, destined to take the

* As an example of our addiction at that time to surnames, I mention that I do not recollect his Christian name.

place of Jimmy Downs and Harold Eldred in my affections. These new-comers were homely folk, a sample of the ordinary men of England, who were not awed by their new surroundings. Ready to learn and to respect the service of those who had already seen so much that was still hidden from them, they were quickly to be admitted to this new society and made to feel at home. Two other members of the group I remember well, though they never entered the inner circle of my acquaintanceship. One was Broome, probably in his thirties—he seemed old to us—a tubby, short, good-natured chap, whose great love for his missis beamed habitually from his open countenance. He came from t'Potteries and ended most of his sentences with the phrase ther knowst'. The other was young Harkins, open, frank and full of *joie de vivre*, destined to become one of the most popular members of the company and a N.C.O. capable of leadership without sacrificing that popularity.

In search of an ephemeral cleanliness we were marched to the baths at Reninghelst, and there were given a glimpse of another army world, for this gay little village, far enough back from the line to be reasonably safe, was simply bubbling over with headquarters officers and personalities. There, in an improvised theatre, our Divisional Concert Party were billing special performances. But the place was too crowded with brass-hats to be comfortable for mere privates.

Back in camp we were that afternoon given an impromptu turn by the enemy. As usual, our balloons were up in strength, some very near. Enemy artillery did some preliminary sniping with shrapnel shells, which invariably missed, but burst uncomfortably low for our peace of mind. Suddenly a German plane appeared out of the blue and made an abortive attack upon the balloons. The speed with which our artillery came into action must have disconcerted him, as he climbed steeply heavenwards. Then the plane seemed to drop out of control away from the expanding black shrapnel patches stippling the sky above him. There was a great shout from the watching troops among the tents, when to our amazement the machine suddenly leapt out of its apparent nose-dive and, now at low altitude and at great speed, the aviator made his escape before our gunners could recover from their surprise and disappointment.

On 4th July the tale went round that 'the man had called to read the meter'. It was the Divisional Gas Officer, resplendent with a dark green band round his hat, who had come to inspect our box respirators, which he did quietly and withdrew without comment. The days of the specialist were dawning, though this had little significance to us at the time!

That same afternoon we marched over to line the main road and give a suitable welcome to the royal car containing H.M. King George V and H.R.H. the Prince of Wales on their way back from the trenches. The fact that this ceremony had been laid on did not detract one bit from the measure of admiration displayed by the ranks at the risks taken by the royal visitors. We found it difficult to understand anyone voluntarily entering those areas of woe and destruction. After all, a chance shell . . .

* * *

When I next made an entry in my diary we were in M-Saps, positioned somewhere to the left of Hill 60, where, as we well knew, the line had been pushed forward during the Messines Battle. Our journey up during the early morning had been uneventful, but now, down in the dark, dank tunnels under the ground, the reverberations of enemy shell-bursts indicated too clearly that we had come to a pretty hot shop. We had been brought in for a short spell to relieve another unit of our 23rd Division, which still held part of the line. An account of the comparatively uneventful week that followed provides a representative picture of what it was like in an active part of the line, such as the Salient still was, although so much pressure had been taken off it by the recent advance on the right flank.

After a night in the unnerving gloom of the sap, feeling apprehensively the trembling turmoil without, we took over an old front-line position known as Canada Street. No. 6 Platoon was assigned to the former German support line and our team was occupying a German strong-point, a square-built structure with walls of concrete at least four feet thick, but with its entrance now disconcertingly facing the enemy. This 'back' front door led into a low passage trench, which circled round and joined the former support position. The dug-out had been used as a heavy machine-gun post, with its field of fire over the two enemy defence lines, now behind us. Debris of its late occupants littered the opening—machine-gun belts, ammunition boxes, equipment, all kinds of rubbish. Inside on the right there was a small rickety table, while to the left were the sleeping quarters divided horizontally by a shelf so as to afford accommodation for six. For a normal team this would have been sufficient, but on the present occasion there were ten: six members of the team, the platoon's Lewis-gun N.C.O., Sergeant McKay, who was relieving Corporal Goffee, and three raw members of the new draft. I found my place precariously on top of the table, which swayed ominously every time I moved. The space under the table had been stacked with Stokes mortar canisters containing sufficient explosive to blow the entire trench sector to smithereens. I was not happy on my uncomfortable couch and for a while I toyed with the idea of sleeping outside. The three newcomers blocked up the passage and looked bewildered, as well they might, for they had suddenly been pitchforked into a world which had hardly any relationship with their former reality.

During the day our job was to lie low and get as much sleep as we could: at night we took the gun out to the corner of a disused communication trench about forty yards in front of our main trench. The trench trickled away towards the enemy's new position, but it was blocked with rubbish at our vantage-point and had been adjudged reasonably secure against surprise attack. As a matter of fact, we had a good field of fire which commanded a long section of the shallow trench as it meandered away into No-man's-land.

In this part of the line, which hinged on to the recent advance, the German positions were now difficult to pinpoint. They were thought to be as far as six hundred yards away over to the left, where there was a large wood. The Salient's left sector still swept away behind us, so that at night, with the continual activity in that part of the line, where the Germans were obviously jumpy about their own position, we had the impression of being menaced on three sides. Directly ahead of us a thin tongue of shattered woodland jutted out into No-man's-land from the right, and was said to be occupied by our troops, although no activity was apparent in that direction.

Our first night out in front was a quiet one in our immediate sector, though we did not feel very happy in our somewhat isolated and not very defensible position. Occasionally an officer came round to see that we were on the alert, but for the rest of the time we felt very much alone, amidst a network of abandoned trenches over which strange spirits seemed to brood. Not that it was a conspicuously quiet night. Our artillery continued to pound the enemy-held wood over on the left. On the left sector, in our rear, fantastic activity continued throughout the night, the Very lights outlining clearly the dark ridge below which our positions were situated. At one stage a call upon our artillery was made by a new kind of SOS rocket which was apparently being tried out. This consisted of a small parachute suspending three lights whose colours could be varied in accordance with a special code. This had the advantage of staying in the air much longer than the ordinary single rockets, but it must have had practical disadvantages, for I do not remember seeing it used later. At another time the tell-tale sparks from the tail of a heavy German *minnewerfer* preceded terrific explosions on that part of the line. My senior companions had many tales of hair-breadth escapes from these missiles, whose advent could be roughly judged. They could only be used when the trenches were fairly close together and we were glad of the gap we knew to exist beyond our present positions.

During the following day we were warned to lie low and not show the least movement. The roads up to the line had been heavily barraged during the night, preventing the arrival of our rations. Thus we were hungry, thirsty and tired for our second night's vigil. It was an active night everywhere, with shells falling all over the area, one or two burst very near emphasising the flimsy nature of our so-called strong-point. Once again the left sector put up a non-stop show and we felt sorry for the troops holding the line there. A new phenomenon appeared as a series of snakelike lights which literally wriggled in swarms down on to the long-suffering ridge. Even my well-informed companions had no acceptable interpretation of this new terror, and this was another offensive means that I was not to meet again.

As the night wore on the enemy artillery became more and more active on our sector, concentrating mainly on the trench behind us, which no doubt the Germans took for our main position, but dropping some shells near our post. Of course, they had every inch of the ground mapped and it was a question of assessing which posts we were actually holding in strength. Unfortunately for us, the N.C.O. who was an excellent fellow and very well liked, lacked the corporal's battle experience and was jumpy throughout the night. At last he decided to go to company headquarters for further instructions, leaving the Number One in charge. The latter had never before found himself in a position of responsibility in such circumstances and we felt leaderless in the developing emergency. We crouched at the bottom of the trench arguing what should be done. Some wanted to return to the main trench before daylight came to disclose our position, one of the younger members even threatened to go back on his own. I made no bones about supporting the stand-fast party. It was so obviously our duty to hold the post pending further orders. Moreover, I had the feeling that we were no more vulnerable where we were than we would be in the trench.

The argument continued and at last our temporary leader went over to the scuttle group. The virtually leaderless team fled precipitately towards the front line. I knew this was wrong, and although as frightened as the rest would have stayed, which, of course, would have been pointless without the gun. Always at such moments in the stress of battle I found my reason struggling strenuously against the fearful temptation to run. This merely pin-points the truth that in war the soldier must know what he is about and have a real sense of his duty if he is not to give way to panic.

As we tore for the trench a regular rain of shells churned up the ground around us and I cannot understand why none of us was hurt. Just before our arrival a direct hit had registered on the junction of the trench, blowing a tremendous gap into it. It was at this very moment that I discerned, through the smoke, C.Q.M.S. Fail, who, having managed to get through with supplies during the night, was actually carrying a box of Mills bombs through the turmoil and looking as though he was enjoying it. There were such men!

The situation in the line was chaotic. Cries from the wounded intermingled with shouts that the enemy was attacking. We were probably lucky not to have been shot down by our own comrades during our hasty retreat. Almost immediately we blundered into our platoon leaders, Second-Lieutenant Edwards and Sergeant Rhodes, who asked us what the hell we were doing out of position, while the former immediately set about accompanying us back. My knees almost gave way at the mere thought of having to return through the tornado, and I was even more intensely annoyed at having been involved in the withdrawal.

We progressed now with difficulty, for the shelling had increased, a barrage falling all along our line. The officer decided to halt us at a bend in the trench some way short of our original position. Out in front the fumes from the German shells, curling across the ground, obscured our view. Anything could be happening!

While I crouched, with the shells bursting in all directions yet fortuitously failing to register a direct hit on this piece of trench, I watched the lieutenant's face. It showed no sign of fear, but instinctively I knew he was afraid. Both he and our platoon sergeant were much of the same type: strict in discipline, imperturbable and soldierly at all times, but too reserved to be popular or even to seek popularity. Although the general opinion was that the ribbons which they both wore for the recent engagement had 'come up with the rations', it was nevertheless conceded that these were men of the right type, leaders to be depended upon in a tight corner. In battle such men, with the knack of instilling confidence, are as rocks in a sea of indecision. Our animal instinct is to run: those who have the will to stand are already on the way to victory—or death. That night at least I was being given a valuable lesson in psychology.

The night's strafe died down at last without Fritz appearing in person and we were ordered to withdraw. It was nearly daylight when we reached our dug-out. In the trench near by our Captain West stood nonchalantly scanning the enemy positions, apparently unaware of the easy target he was offering to the sniper taking up his watch with the dawn. Remarking, in the tone of small talk about a drawing-room incident, that the Boche had obviously packed up for the time being, he quietly withdrew, while we crept thankfully into our concrete refuge.

When I awoke from a fitful slumber on my precarious couch the sun was streaming down into the passageway outside. It seemed a pity to be forced to spend another day cooped up when all was so serene outside. Yet the recollection of one or two bullets which had spanged over the breastwork on our first morning was sufficient warning to be wary of appearances. One by one the others awoke and our first eager impulse was to attack the rations whose arrival my fleeting vision of the quartermaster had betokened.

During the morning I walked out into the shadow of the opening to stretch my legs, keeping low behind the barrier of earth which still masked the door. All was quiet. A man sat in the doorway inspecting his shirt, while the others either dozed or wrote in the sunrays which had turned the interior into a study in black and white. I began to clean my rifle. At this very moment, some miles away in enemy territory, our precise map reference was being carefully checked by the artillery 'mathematicians'. Movements in our vicinity had been sufficient to indicate to enemy observers that we were occupying a post which they themselves had so laboriously constructed. Our first warning came with the low moan of a shell which approached and burst near by.

We hustled into apparent safety. The illusion of security which, despite all previous experience, we were ever ready to nurture, was immediately shattered. The next shell, following on the heels of the first from a twin gun, burst with a roar above us. The dug-out trembled as acrid fumes, billowing in through the door-opening, blotted out the light and made us gasp for breath. The sergeant, awakened from a peaceful doze on the upper shelf, sat up quickly and bumped his head against the concrete ceiling. 'Quick, quick,' he shouted, 'the dug-out's fallin' in.' We laughed uproarously, as though he had cracked the joke of all jokes. Tension relaxed.

A few more shell-bursts followed, none so uncomfortably close, and all was quiet again. We had to dig our way through the earth and debris by which the opening had been choked. All the concrete blocks round the doorway were badly pitted with shrapnel marks. It was not, however, until we had got out and inspected the shell's main impact that we realised how narrow our escape had been, and we were overwhelmed with thankfulness. The dug-out had been hit fair and square above the door, a direct hit if ever there was one. The blast had cleared away all the accumulated rubbish and barbed wire from the top and eaten out a considerable chunk of the concrete. Our escape had been little short of miraculous. The marksmanship was a tribute to the enemy artillery, for to hit so decisively a buried target in this way was in any case the outside chance. The dug-out's survival from such a tremendous blow at its weakest spot was in itself a great tribute to the German engineers.

The sergeant crawled round to the trench to seek further orders. Of course, we had to stay put. That night it was our turn to take over a twenty-four-hour post out in No-man's-land, and we were now inclined to regard this as the lesser evil.

It was quiet when we relieved the isolated post at stand-to. Our predecessors were only too obviously pleased to depart. The post was situated in a shallow section of trench, one end of which, in the direction of the enemy positions, abutted a large shell-hole, half-filled with water. It was roughly covered with iron girders and old sandbags, providing little more than protection from shrapnel. But it merged into the surrounding vast muck-heap of the battlefield and no doubt movement alone would give the position away when daylight came. The shelter itself was hardly more than six feet long and so narrow that our knees touched as we sat four a side, as if in a railway carriage.

It was impossible to stir outside in daylight for any reason. There was quite insufficient cover. To regain our own trench we should have had to cross eighty to a hundred yards of ground in full view. I was perhaps fortunate in occupying one of the seats abutting the shell-hole, opposite a corporal from another platoon who had been deputed to take charge of us. Over my left shoulder I could discern our own trench standing out clearly along the skyline, while somewhere in front of me, but still leftwards, was situated the enemy position. In front but to the right, much nearer now, was the tongue of wood which we now knew definitely to be occupied by our own troops, though not of our battalion. There was a break here in the continuity of our line, and our job, in case of enemy attack, was to prevent a thrust between the two positions, which certainly would have been a weak spot had the enemy been aware of it. As far as I could see at the time our mission would have been something of a forlorn hope, as the enemy barrage, unless it missed us entirely, would almost certainly have settled accounts straight away.

We had been given unusually generous rations to bring out with us and eating was one of the ways of passing the monotonous hours. Not that any special effort was called for on our part. We were all young with animal appetites, sharpened by our rigorous life and the general meagreness of our diet. I can remember few occasions during those hectic years when a good square meal would not have been welcome—and I was not the sort that ever considered eating one of the special pleasures of life. Thus we ate, and we read, and some wrote, adding to the stream of loving letters that brought heart to fatherless and sonless homes during the long months of waiting.

I found it difficult to keep my mind clear of the most frightful thoughts, and the general conversation indicated that I was not alone in my fears. We did not relish the long vigil before us. The waste around was still, almost as the grave it so closely resembled, for it was scattered with the dead bodies and shattered hopes of the once-vigorous youth of two great nations whose friendship could have saved the future of our civilisation. I was sorely afraid all through that July day. Suppose our predecessors had given the position away by careless movement? One shell would be enough. Indeed, looking through the low opening, as from a belvedere over the stagnant water, I could not understand why we were not easily seen.

The smokers moaned because they could not smoke and the corporal had to exert all his authority to restrain them. Then it began to rain. The shell-hole soon became even more of a pond. Water dripped upon us through the flimsy roof. Heavy clouds and rain-mist obscured the horizon and a clammy chilliness settled all around us. Cooped in our sodden trap it is not easy to exaggerate the weight of depression that fell upon us. After a time the rain did abate, leaving a Scotch mist wrapped like a cloak about the lines.

Then among the broken trees not far ahead we saw a tall figure, moving like a shepherd with the aid of a simple staff, a shepherd looking for his lost sheep! We recognised the brigadier-general, alone and quite unconcerned. On a routine visit to the firing positions—a rare visitor to such places, one should add—he had no doubt decided to take advantage of the comparative obscurity to dispense with the disadvantages of trench travel. After all, who there could prevent him, if he had the mind? We observed him with fearful expectancy lest he should spot us and wander over to investigate. He meandered thus for some time; the mists continued to hide him from enemy observation and at last, to our great relief, he returned to earth unharmed.

Later in the afternoon, when the mists had cleared, a lively bombardment commenced from both sides. Enemy shells seemed to be feeling about No-man's-land for something. We offered a sitting target and could not see why anyone but ourselves could be their quarry. Spent shrapnel and shell splinters moaned into our flimsy cover. A near burst in the pond drove in a wave of slimy water through the opening. It was terrifying, and we felt worse from the knowledge that we could not run—unwise as that would have been in any case—to ease our tensions.

That was indeed a day to try the strongest nerves. Yet there were also comparatively minor ills to add to the cumulative weight of our discomfort. The ubiquitous lice had us at special disadvantage and were not slow in increasing their frolics. We were beset by an itch that was barely tolerable except when fear overshadowed all bodily discomforts. A man of the recent draft and consequently new to all this—his name was Venus, it I recollect aright—was affected more than most, and an upset stomach, understandable in all the circumstances, found the pressures of nature too much for him. So far urination had been practicable through the use of a rusty mess tin picked out of the debris the night before, but this was another matter. Despite the general disapprobation, he did his best in all the circumstances, but splashes of excreta falling across our miniature food store put further eating from my mind for the rest of the day!

At last the dusk began to fall and the corporal released us from our vow of inactivity. It was a wonderful sensation to be able to stretch one's cramped limbs in the low trench leading to the post. Shortly the clanking of equipment denoted the welcome approach of our relief and we were glad to return to our strong-point, there to sleep with little thought of its vulnerability well into the new day.

That night our sister battalion, the 10th Northumberlands,

relieved us and we withdrew into close support in the Canada Street saps. Those galleries were already in a rotting state, the timbers seeming to threaten collapse at any moment. Everything wept with moisture. A fetid smell of decaying matter rose from the gutters, which were frequently used for unauthorised purposes. I occupied a dilapidated bunk on which I could stretch at full length and was willing to overlook much for this comfort and apparent safety.

But our troubles were far from over. In this support position our function was to provide working parties which were required to maintain the fighting positions in a state of minimal efficiency. This had been the original British front line, only a stone's throw from the enemy's main trench, and a particularly hot-shop, if the almost loving reminiscences of my companions of those seemingly far-off times, of but a few months earlier, were to be credited. And credit them I did, with shuddering relief that our new evils, if just as deadly, were more impersonal in their implications.

Among these reminiscences I was told how Fritz at Christmas-time had caught the company unawares in a bombing raid, which had resulted in casualties on both sides and—as they put it—the accidental decorating with a Military Medal of one of the company's lance-corporals, whose habitual pomposity had made him the butt for the company's somewhat uncharitable humour. I remember him well, though I forget his name. He frequently acted as orderly corporal and was for some time leader of the battalion's brass band. His pirouetting and ineffectual self-assurance in the latter position went far to explain the ridicule that he invariably drew, though I doubt whether he ever himself realised that his activities were received with other than the seriousness that was their due. After all, it wasn't a bad band!

As we lay in our bunks we could hear the racket above. The galleries reverberated as the shells thumped into the receptive earth. Last night's ration party had been badly hit on the way and we went hungry until a later party got through during the afternoon. At dusk I went with a working party to draw planks from a dump at Ration Farm. These were required by the Royal Engineers to repair the galleries. Our way lay across a hollow below the ridge which, although hidden from enemy observation, was too obviously a communications route to be left long without bombardment. As we came back we were caught in the barrage and there is nothing more tiresome and ludicrous than trying to run across shell-torn ground with a bulky plank swaying up and down across one's shoulder. To make matters worse, having been chased off the normal duck-board track, there were disused trenches to cross. For this purpose the planks provided useful bridges but, under the stress of bombardment, I completely failed to see the humour of the situation when those following behind tried to use the board I had put down for this purpose. An impartial observer—if such could have existed—would have been quite unable to appreciate the spontaneous indignation which I felt at this, after all, quite sensible arrangement. But I had my plank to deliver!

Every kind of shell seemed to be bursting over the area, while the ridge ahead—and our objective—was being mercilessly hammered by enemy 5.9s. We waited a little way back behind a pile of waste and rubble until a momentary slackening of the fire made it possible to run to the sap opening and safety.

There were no casualties on this occasion, which surprised me at the time, and I find it no less amazing in retrospect. But the effect upon our nerves was shattering and we waited in fearful dread throughout the next day in anticipation of the night's task. On that occasion an early party was caught not far from the opening and terribly mangled, the survivors coming back in disorder. The next party, to which I had been assigned, was lined up in the semi-darkness of the entrance passage awaiting its turn. Heavy shells continued to rain down, shaking the whole world in which we were buried, and screaming the most awful fear into our hearts. Some fell so close to the sheltered opening that the bright glow of the burst lit up the seeping sandbags around us. The absolute safety of the burrow intensified the contrasting terror outside. As the minutes ticked slowly by the burden of waiting became less and less supportable. The clatter went on, as it seemed, interminably. Our officer stood undecidedly watching the opening for an opportunity to take the party forth, as fearful no doubt as the rest of us, but steeled to do his duty at any cost when the moment should come.

Unexpectedly, word arrived that there had already been too

many casualties, and the task was cancelled. The joy with which this news was received was itself painful. Once an order had been given it was most unusual for it to be rescinded. We had come to feel that the powers that be were impervious to the dangers that beset the mere actors in this endless tragedy. The normal truth was that the whole business was usually too vast and incoherent for those above to be able to react in time, but on this occasion the enemy bombardment had continued long enough for information about the casualties to accumulate at battalion headquarters, with the result I have recounted.

In the daylight the occasional calls of nature made it necessary to mount the flight of stairs to the unoccupied trench above. These steps actually led up from a spot near my sleeping-place, bending narrowly through a sufficient depth of sheltering earth. That afternoon I chose a quiet moment for my expedition to the outer world, but I was in a bad state of nerves as I stepped out into the open. The sun was shining brightly. Over the parados there spread before me a wonderful panorama stretching way back beyond Ypres. The shattered city, the reflecting surface of the Zillebeke Bund and every detail of the flat countryside stood out clearly. For a moment I forgot my fears in the wonder of that magnificent picture in the warm sunshine and I realised in a flash, as I had never done before, how it had been possible for Fritz to fire down so terrifyingly on all those night working parties. Occupying as the Germans did the investing ridges, it was a marvel that we had been able to resist them so successfully.

The latrine, two empty biscuit tins let conveniently into the sides of a small recess cut out of the trench, was that afternoon the assembly place of a myriad of buzzing flies, whose noise seemed sufficient to drown the premonitory scream of an approaching shell. Despite the view and the sunshine I had little inclination to tarry in such an unsavoury and dangerous spot!

That night the working parties were again cancelled, but for very different reasons. Early the following morning the Durhams were to carry out a bombing stunt, which was reported later to have been completely successful. Enemy fire concentrated upon our positions during the raid, and some of our own people were caught outside the saps. We had already heard that during the previous day another shell had hit our former concrete emplacement, killing all its occupants. The earlier hit must have taken all the resistance out of the structure.

In the midst of the turmoil a Yorkshire battalion appeared, as if from nowhere, to relieve us, but the Lewis-gun teams were to stand fast for the time being. Orders were slow in coming, day seemed to be on the point of breaking and we feared having to spend another day in the saps, or, alternatively, being spotted by the enemy as we left during daylight. At long last our release came and, burdened with guns and ammunition, we literally fled across the open into the morning light. Yet the world remained as silent as the grave until we had reached the shelter of the communication trench leading down through Zillebeke, and after all those recent bombardments that silence seemed a miracle for which there could be no explanation.

The silence did not last long and the Salient returned to its normal state of unrest, but the trench, which took us alongside the waters of the lake, afforded good shelter. We were able to take necessary rests in comparative safety. With us were some company runners who had also stayed behind and two lightly wounded members who, as was usual in such circumstances, were making us truly jealous by discussing the anticipated joys of a short spell in hospital away from it all. Enemy shells were now falling in all directions and things were decidedly lively. It was a strange sensation to be viewing the old Salient in broad daylight, still dead to movement, but relieved of much of its original burden of terror. A few weeks earlier to have used this trench in daylight would have exposed us to enemy bullets from the low ridge we had just left.

As we neared the end of the Bund we witnessed a sight rare enough under conditions of trench warfare, a sight no longer seen in these days of complete mechanisation, one indeed that caused us to halt with surprise. The ammunition wagons of some field battery, caught by the daylight much nearer the line than was healthy, had thrown caution to the winds and were galloping away across the open towards Ypres at full speed. The wagons seemed literally to cleave through the air behind the straining horses, which their drivers were lashing frantically. We were spell-bound by this scene of magnificent war with a pictorial quality such as one saw in the picture-books and such as we rarely experienced.

The enemy gunners must have been as surprised as we were, for the galloping train disappeared in a cloud of dust and no shell had burst in its direction!

At Shrapnel Corner, of dire fame, an impatiently waiting battalion limber relieved us of our guns and ammunition, while we continued the journey on foot. The roads were strangely deserted; here and there derelict buildings stood by the wayside. We had the world to ourselves; but not quite, for over the horizon behind us an enemy observation balloon hung threateningly in the sky. I feared lest at any moment our departure should be speeded by the whining approach we knew so well. For once imagination was raising unwarranted fears; common sense should have told me that the enemy could not afford to waste ammunition on any piffling group of moving men that might come within their vision. They were looking for movements that promised more profitable quarries. Weary but in good heart we rejoined the company in Mic Mac Camp in time for breakfast.

For a further week we tarried on the edge of the battle zone, glad enough for this modest respite, for the battalion had suffered a hundred casualties during the recent 'quiet' spell in the line, a sufficiently heavy toll for such a routine operation. The area of the camps, a comparatively narrow band running parallel to the front, was increasing in activity almost daily. Everywhere there was movement, comings and goings, purposeful no doubt, though few could interpret that purpose. Here and there amidst all the military improvisation civilian buildings were scattered, sometimes shattered but frequently intact, including some windmills, their sails protruding above the army hutments. Among the ordinary batteries, which were positioned all over the place, there was somewhere an immense gun whose discharge overshadowed all others: its shell left with the noise of an express train followed by a fountain of vapour which columned high into the air. One had no wish to be near the receiving end!

Belgian citizens still hung on in small numbers here and there, tilling as carefully as ever the militarily unoccupied fields just as though there were no untoward happenings in the vicinity. Their continued presence was a fruitful spur to rumour. Spies were detected everywhere and the possible use of the sails of an intact windmill often excitedly discussed. There was probably little basis for such fantasies, but, of course, we had plenty of time for thought and talk; in the absence of sufficient informed news, rumours were self-perpetuating. Such important developments as the recent retreat at Nieuport, where our left flank ran into the North Sea, and the enemy's increasing submarine attacks on our sealines could not be seen in their proper perspective.

Thus we paraded and worked and waited amidst the bustle of preparation for a new battle. The observation balloons went up all along the front as a matter of course and were attacked again and again. Enemy planes snooped across the sky, giving us the impression that our own aircraft were less effective than they actually were. In the evenings those who had money went in search of the estaminet from which came sounds of laughter and the clinking of glasses, and not infrequently the smell of fried eggs, which all enjoyed as a welcome change from army rations. One evening I found myself in Reninghelst, visiting the 'Follies', an amusing show put on by one of the divisional concert parties.

One day we were employed in sorting over stocks of small-arms ammunition to pick out certain brands of American manufacture which had been found faulty and disinclined to go off. On another occasion we paraded to try out the Yukon pack, a contraption fitting across one's back and so designed as to distribute loads more evenly. We were informed that it would be used during future offensives, but we were not impressed. Apart from making the carrier more conspicuous, we wondered what would happen to the poor devil who went to earth with a loaded Yukon pack strapped to him. I do not recollect, in fact, that this contraption was widely adopted.

To me personally the most important incident of that period was my 'discovery' of Harrison's pomade. Corporal Goffee occasionally received from a kind aunt one of those miscellaneous parcels that brought joy to the more fortunate of us. His parcels always included a small tin of the pomade, which the corporal could not use and always gave away, although eager recipients were few. Thus it was that I gratefully received a tin on this occasion. The purpose of the pomade, a herbalistic ointment, was to kill lice. I was told straight away by the others that the stuff was greasy, smelly and calculated to make one itch even more than the chats. Anything, I felt, would be better than the loathsome lice. Greasy the ointment certainly was, but I placed a greasy shirt far down the scale in my catalogue of evils, nor was the smell disagreeable. As it happened, my skin proved impervious to it, while the lice certainly did not! I became an addict and I hastened to ensure that in future my mother should keep me in good supply. I used it throughout the rest of my service and for me henceforth the pest was reduced to bearable proportions. The pomade certainly killed and even prevented the hatching of the clusters of eggs in the seams of one's clothes, but, of course, it could only keep at bay the hordes of invaders that came in from without, for everywhere clothes and sleeping-places were infested. Yet my 'conversion' seemed to make little difference to the others whose rooted prejudices against the messy stuff prevented their giving it a fair trial.

We bathed in a swimming-pool set up artificially in a neighbouring field; we did a little shooting on an improvised range, the only way of keeping up our marksmanship in that mainly non-shooting war; we practised with the Lewis gun, the newcomers receiving much instruction from the experienced members of the team. One day when I fired the gun for the first time, an occasion always accompanied by a certain amount of tension, its ease of manoeuvre gave me great confidence. These practices had the virtue of keeping me off many of the working parties into the battle zone which other members of the company were experiencing.

They brought back disturbing tales and one in particular of a shaking experience at a place on the canal known as Lock-8. It was there, too, that on another occasion a party from the 10th Battalion were badly cut up. I did go one day with a party to move shells from an artillery dump near Hallebast Corner. The shells were stacked in large blocks laid out like a miniature town with gangways forming regular streets between. The type we had to manhandle was only just about within our carrying capacity and it was a very fatiguing task. During the process I could not help wondering what would be the effect of a direct hit from one of those stray shells which now and again literally dropped out of the sky. Dumps did go up from time to time, and were a most desirable target if they could be found. Their permanent guardians did not seem to be much perturbed, for they were stationed in 'safe' areas and had no wish to change with the 'poor bloody infantry'.

On the 22nd July we were glad to march back again to the old camp at Le Thieushouk, re-entering the little hamlet with our drum-and-fife band blaring away in front, our musicians being accompanied in great style by a shaggy goat, which had been only recently 'won' and pressed, somewhat reluctantly, into the office of regimental mascot. The spectacle of our pompous band-master being dragged by the goat at the head of the column caused a good deal of mirth in the ranks.

Orders were immediately issued for a major clean-up; we were hard put to remove traces of the recent sojourn in the battle zone. The colonel and the major came round on different occasions to inspect our kits, laid out in a carefully determined order so devised as to facilitate the check and keep us up to scratch. Then we had another visit from the divisional general (Babbington), following all the usual rather childish preliminaries and with all the officers and N.C.O.s in a fine state of nerves.

There were lighter occasions: as, for example, one afternoon when No. 6 Platoon won a bomb-throwing competition—owing little, I fear, to my own mediocre contribution. Later the same day the battalion engaged in an intercompany sports tournament in which we all participated. It happened that 'B' Company was blessed with some very good peacetime athletes and our victory, despite the rabbits, was largely a foregone conclusion. Westgarth, our Section's Number One was a good amateur sprinter, while in the company we had Quickval, the brigade boxing champion, who was so good that he had been barred from the competitions lest other entrants should be completely discouraged.

Some evenings I went on lonely rambles, glad to get away from all compulsions. I went down between the summer hedgerows, through Godwaersvelde to the pretty little village of Eecke, recognising with delight many butterflies of species I already knew in England fluttering in the sunlight. Just before the outbreak of war, as a youth of seventeen in July 1914, I was holidaying in the neighbourhood of the New Forest with an accomplished entomologist who was a sergeant in the peacetime

Territorials, and whom I was never to see again. That is how it was in those days. I saw on this present occasion a green-veined white, a small heath, a tortoise-shell and an unidentified fritillary, and for a moment imagined myself back in the old sane world, away from evil reality and into the land of sweetest dreams. I was particularly taken by a delightful little peacock, which seemed smaller than our English butterfly, but even prettier as its gay wings sparkled in the sunshine. Such moments of complete release were as rare as they were welcome, for even when it was not visually present the war brooded continuously over our souls.

One day we awoke to sweltering sunshine and marched to the divisional baths at Meteren in shirt-sleeves. At this very moment the weather suddenly changed, one of the many such changes during that variable summer of 1917, and our bath was anticipated by a deluge that soaked us to the skin. In my tent that evening I felt very unwell, but this was just a passing chill, for I was young and, whether I liked it or not, the open-air life obviously agreed with me. The next day, the 30th July, brought the good news that the division was being relieved at last and there was the prospect of a good spell away from the line to refit and recuperate for the next assignment. There was more singing than usual in the camp that night. It was a most appropriate moment to be going on our summer holidays.

Plans for an extended Flanders offensive had gone ahead steadily, although their execution continued in doubt for some time. An important development adverse to it had been the French commander's inability to provide the co-operation that the plan originally presupposed: strongly in favour were the reports coming to hand of the severe effects of the heavy casualties sustained by the Germans in recent battles. But the War Cabinet in London were difficult to convince and, in fact, their final approval did not arrive till two days after the preparatory bombardment had been initiated.

There had been serious pressures from many directions. Shipping losses, though now beginning to fall away from the high peak reached in May and June, were still very heavy. Troubles in the French army, though subsiding, were far from over. Italian pressure for military reinforcement from the Western Front to enable them to carry out a decisive offensive against the Austrians was to some extent favoured by the politicians. On the Russian front a brave attempt by the constitutional Kerensky Government to renew the offensive was decisively frustrated by the Germans, with the result that the Bolsheviks achieved control in Petrograd and further Russian co-operation in the war was at an end. To cap everything the spoiling offensive by the Germans at Nieuport on 10th July, which has already been mentioned, postponed the prospect of a thrust from the coast by the British Fourth Army which had been an important part of the original scheme. As a result, the modified offensive was to be a step-by-step operation not differing greatly from the war of attrition now favoured—characteristically—by the new French commander, General Pétain. No doubt there were very good reasons for the gap of six weeks since the Battle of Messines, but the loss of time was to cost dear.

The first stage of the Third Battle of Ypres aimed at advancing the British line to the higher ground facing the northern flank of the old Salient which had not been shifted in the Messines battle. Sir Douglas Haig hoped initially to reach the ridge extending from Stirling Castle by Passchendaele, Staden and Clercken to near Dixmude, which would again open the way to the coastal thrust planned by the Fourth Army, now holding the coastal positions, with a Franco-Belgian force between it and the Fifth Army, to which main responsibility for the opening of the Ypres offensive had been assigned. Although the ridge was not a high one, the ground was full of obstacles to an attacking force.

The preliminary bombardment opened up on 18th July. At that time the beginning of the offensive was fixed for the 25th July, but, owing to unexpected losses in guns and the non-arrival of certain heavy artillery, followed by a run of dull cloudy weather impeding observation, two successive postponements, each of three days, put back the date to 31st July. Haig himself was greatly annoyed by these delays and apprehensive, with good reason, about the forecasts of wet weather early in August which were coming in.

*Thus the new offensive began on 31st July, the very day on which the 11th Northumberland Fusiliers reached their training area around the small village of Quelmes.**

* Continued in next Historical Note: see p. 121.

CHAPTER IV

PREPARATION FOR BATTLE

On the following day our orders arrived and we entrained at Caestre, where I saw a detachment of the new Chinese Labour Corps, about the employment of which there had been a good deal of controversy at home. They were hard at work unloading trucks and one might well wonder what was going through their minds at finding themselves thus occupied in a completely alien land so far from home. I do not recollect where we detrained, but there was still a march of ten kilometres from the railhead to the pretty but sleepy little village of Quelmes. We ought to have been elated, but, whether because of a depressing change in the weather or my personal feeling of being off colour, our new address did not seem very attractive. There was much grumbling in the ranks that evening.

We were billeted in a farm, not indeed a Bairnsfather farm, but on the contrary an up-to-date establishment using the latest American farm machinery. Between the main buildings on one side and the dwellings of the workers on the other there was a truly vast courtyard, much of which consisted of a messy midden. The whole place seemed to be overflowing with prosperity, a fact which somehow we resented. Our billet was a large barn, a regular sieve of a barn which let in both wind and the rain. This structure, the worst serviced of the whole farm, was actually pierced by the roadway which gave access to the centre court. Many inches of mud had accumulated around the entrance, and this we had to negotiate when entering and leaving the billet. Chickens and inquisitive ducks waddled in to inspect our kits; wallowing in the slime near by were immense porkers whose smell was not much to our liking. The officers were billeted in the main building on the far side of the courtyard, where also a temporary estaminet had been set up to sell *vin rouge* and further increase the prosperity of the establishment.

It rained almost continuously for the next three days. The

billet was clammy, time hung heavily on our hands, despite efforts to channel our energies by giving us small-arms ammunition to clean. Our spirits dropped to zero. It was at this moment, on 2nd August, that I received my greatest blow during those sad years. The post contained many congratulatory messages on my twentieth birthday, now only two days ahead, but there was a letter from Grace, which otherwise would have been more than welcome, which contained the news of the recent death somewhere in the Salient of her brother and my childhood friend, Eddie Collins, one of the many promising lives blotted out in that awful catastrophe. He had been overseas for but a few months. A bombardier in the Royal Garrison Artillery, he had been killed immediately when a gas shell registered a direct hit on the dug-out he was occupying, surely an outside chance of all chances in that war. He was not an intellectual, had not shone at school, for he was a doer rather than a thinker: he was ambitious and would surely have done well in life. I had envied him his keenness, and now he was dead; I who had seen so much death could not believe it. How I replied to that letter from one whose love I hoped so ardently to win, I cannot say. It must have been a poor pained effort. At least he had a grave, such as Eldred and others were not to have, and this I was to visit some years after the war in the Tyne Cot Cemetery, kept in admirable order through the efforts of our War Graves Commission.

* * *

After a few days the rain began to ease up and we were able to stretch our legs. The battalion ranged over the hills, practising the attack. We felt better. Captain West rode his horse, not altogether to the manner born, for he was, I know, a member of the professional class. We were all immensely amused when he handed over his steed to each of the platoon leaders in turn to have a go, which they did awkwardly and without enthusiasm.

One day an immense boar was brought in by farm hands to run loose in the midden and this led to much coarse humour. The farm women, who stood round watching proceedings, must have wondered at our peculiar English attitudes to what to them was too serious a business for fun.

General Plumer came again to look at the division—a sure sign, we thought, that we should soon be on the move once more. And so it proved; for on 9th August we marched away from the somewhat depressing farm, not knowing our destination and, of course, fearing the worst. As it happened we kept among the green fields, passing through Tilques and Zudasques to Serques, there to be billeted in a delightful farm on the banks of a little stream. The company was allotted to a barn, but we gunners accounted ourselves fortunate in being assigned to a clean, tiled cowshed on the opposite side of a little courtyard. This was quite a different type of farm settlement from our last. The stream flowed serenely alongside the courtyard, past a water-mill and on to the village about ten minutes' walk away. Compared with the place at Quelmes, where we had had to use cattle troughs we were well off for washing facilities, always an important factor in assessing a billet.

In this pleasant rural billet the company was to spend a couple of quiet weeks. The amenities were good. We could hire punts on the stream, or visit an excellent rest hut in the village, which was the headquarters of an artillery school. I had known that Eddie had attended such a school not many weeks before and wondered by how little our paths might have failed to cross. There were food shortages among the civilian population and in consequence we were forbidden to buy bread; however, there was a Y.M.C.A. always ready to help us out in other ways, as well as to provide enjoyable concerts from the talent contributed from the units in the area. A member of our own battalion, billed as 'The Yorkshire Comedian', scored a great success with his humorous monologues.

During this time my friendship with Canelle developed rapidly. We were birds of a feather, harbouring similar hopes for the world of after the war. I envied him his prowess in having passed the Second Division examination, a feat I hoped to emulate when the time came. Life would then be assured, and amidst the awful uncertainties of the present such a vision could not but seem a dream of paradise. Canelle, I felt, was out of his element in the ranks and would never settle down to the life as I had done, as something one had to make the best of. On the other hand, I do not think he had the potential drive for leadership and it seemed that he was destined to continue as a fish out of water.

These were indeed carefree days. Yet even as we lazed upon the river bank and propelled the punt along shady banks with an enjoyment rare for that wartime, more deadly activities were being planned for our participation. Authority took us over the fields, practising a new form of open-order advance which they called 'artillery formation', or 'advancing in blobs'. This was a manoeuvre by which a marching column coming under shellfire would break up automatically into small groups to minimise the target without stopping progress.

One night an enemy plane, droning above, dropped bombs in the vicinity, causing damage to a civilian hospital. Before daybreak our quartermaster-sergeant had us out of bed to collect a change of clean underclothing. We still thought the 'clean' garments were too lousy to be worth getting up for and for once C.Q.M.S. Fail was not popular. Perhaps he had been ordered to do this for fear the store should be hit!

Unsettling rumours began to stalk among us, most prominently upon the lips of a corporal who could not resist letting it be known that he was the recipient of 'confidential knowledge'. The aims of our recent exertions were made plain, if we really had been so obtuse as not to have guessed. The battalion was to take part in a major attack in a week or two's time. Within a day or two the forthcoming attack was actually explained to us, in such detail as we had never hitherto experienced. A large-scale advance was shown on the map in a series of objectives, each marked as a coloured line. The map also showed the enemy strong-points which the artillery would deal with *seriatim*, leaving it merely to our mopping-up parties to clear out their defenders. On the following day counter-rumour had it that the projected battle had been cancelled. Instead we were to join the Second Army, which had been severely cut up. We saw no special reason for believing this.

On the 24th of the month all doubts were put to rest when we entrained for the Salient and by the end of the day found ourselves back in Mic Mac Camp, packed like sardines fifty men to each small hut. As if by a wave of a magic wand the green fields of Serques, which we had so recently left, became a sort of impossible Elysian dream, an Arcadian retreat such as could not possibly exist that side of the Channel.

Reports from the front were far from reassuring. Our advance parties told of shocking conditions on the sector chosen for our attack. Dozens of tanks had got bogged down by the mire, and the ground was adjudged as practically impassable. An attacking wave in a recent push went dutifully forward, well shielded by our barrage, and just disappeared without trace into the morass: not a single straggler had crawled back. Our officers, usually so self-assured, found it difficult to talk about the coloured lines as though they represented anything real.

Definite news came on the 27th that the attack would be launched at the end of the week, and we felt a certain relief at knowing the worst. Just about this time a leave party had been announced. It included Golightly of our section, who had not been home for a year. We envied him indeed and would have literally sold our souls for his double good fortune. It was good for him that he was going before the attack, or such was the general opinion, since there was a widespread belief that death came inevitably to those who went into battle when sweating on leave. Golightly left with much chaffing from the rest of us, but with all our good wishes. On the very same day rain began to pour. It went on continuously for forty-eight hours, until water was running into and out of everything.

It was not difficult to imagine the state of the front and this was confirmed by men who went up on briefing parties. The ground out in front was littered with corpses which could not be reached, often held up in grotesque attitudes by the wire and the mud. Enemy shelling was knocking our defence positions to pieces. From these reports it seemed that the terrain, the enemy and now the weather were combining on this front all the worst conditions of both the Salient and the Somme.

The army machine continued to move forward to the appointed day according to plan. On a blackboard map our officers pointed out many of the places that were destined to become key-positions in the Passchendaele agony, with such names as Clapham Junction, Stirling Castle, Polygon and Glencorse Woods. This was followed by a trip down the road towards Poperinghe, where the experts had constructed an immense scale-model of the terrain of the proposed advance. Though we had little stomach for our approaching glory, we certainly appreciated thus being brought into the picture and showed a good deal of interest in the demonstration. It struck me personally as a remarkable piece of work. Ridges and valleys, roads and tracks, trenches and defence works—both British and German—woods and marshes; all the important features were shown in relief, clearly marked and coloured, and on such a scale that we could cross the map by well-defined paths to inspect more closely the points of greatest interest and have them explained in detail. Here was the red line, the first objective, clearly marked; and there, farther ahead, the blue line; while beyond that again was the yellow. Here and there were the enemy strongpoints which would have to be mopped up after our artillery had done with them. On the first line the barrage would halt for twenty minutes while the people over to our right were clearing up a wood. Farther over, a territory to be avoided, were the indefinite wastes of the Nonneboschen, a swamp about which the staff themselves were uncertain. Beyond all this, beginning on the far fringe of the model, where the last ridges trailed away, was the quiet Flemish countryside, with nestling untouched villages, where today the Germans had their billets; and spread out behind the front lay the railheads of Comines, Menin and Roulers, whose names we already knew so well. When we had taken those last heights Fritz would have to go back to his second defence line and—not for the first time in those years of great expectations—the war would be as good as over! The confidence of the staff was colossal and pathetic at the same time. So much had happened before to evoke pessimistic assumptions. And now the rain, again not for the first time in this high summer month, was taking a hand.

On 29th August we moved up to Dickebusch, taking up residence in a camp of tents and bivvies in a large meadow not far from the village. Here were the headquarter camps and horse-lines, the homes of the farriers and ordnance men, and suchlike experts who waited upon the needs of the fighting troops, whose lot they certainly did not envy.

At this time rumour began to run through the camp that we were to lose Captain West, who had volunteered for the Royal

Flying Corps, and we were genuinely distressed. If ever a leader was loved by the troops under him, that leader was the captain. We felt sad at the prospect, yet wished him well in his transfer.

On the following day, which was the anniversary of my first crossing to France, I felt particularly disconsolate. I looked back over a year of discomfort and disillusion; the end seemed as far off as ever and the prospect of another year such as this was barely tolerable. At times I, who was so young and should have been gaining strength and confidence in grappling with an expanding life, felt tired, forlorn and cut off from all the people and things I cared for, immured in a sort of evil cell that was but the antechamber to death. It was only from the feeling that we were with those who were doing their duty and that we were suffering for those whom we had left behind, and for the ideals and future of our country, that any real consolation could be. derived. On this day I remember going with Canelle to the shattered church of Dickebusch, which still retained some of its original style, despite the battering it had received. It was a solace to stand there on hallowed ground with a companion who spoke in cultured voice of life's better things. Such interludes were a rare experience in those days.

On the following afternoon I was sitting at the end of our bivvy writing a letter home when I suddenly became aware of commotion around me. Whistle blasts and cries of 'Stand still' or 'Take cover', rose on all sides and in the air above I saw some half-dozen enemy planes shining like silver in the sunlight. Our anti-aircraft guns opened out with a crash; while, from the surrounding camps, Lewis-gun and rifle fire added to the din. Corporal Goffee, shouting for spare ammunition, rushed the gun to a near-by field kitchen which seemed to provide the handiest stand for firing vertically into the air. It should be added that we had not yet been equipped with sighting aids and equipment for this type of offensive action. The planes were now close and one swooped down to rake the field with machine-gun fire. We flung ourselves to the ground, hoping for the best. No one was hit. Already bombs were dropping on neighbouring camps. Quickly the planes began to wheel and to return very much as they had come, without apparent damage. The noise of battle subsided almost as quickly as it had begun. A daylight raid of this sort had been so unexpected that the audacious airmen had got away with it unscathed.

With us the story was very different. Heavy casualties were reported from all sides. Bombs, which fell in the next field, occupied by a section of Royal Engineers, left a bloody trail across the camp. A number were killed and many seriously wounded. One victim had both his legs blown away. All wounds seem to have been in the legs and lower parts of the body. A bomb which fell on the horse-lines literally tore some of the poor creatures to pieces. One of them dashed across the field with his entrails hanging down. Its awful bellow of pain, in protest against man's inhumanity, was more shocking than all the rest of that afternoon's nightmare.

The bombs had been so contrived as to burst along the ground, as shrapnel marks on posts near this particular tragedy clearly indicated. The hole in the ground made by the explosion was little bigger than a football. These anti-personnel bombs were new to us at the time. They were designed to burst on contact and could be deadly among bivouacs and horse-lines. It was no longer enough just to sprawl upon the ground when under fire. Now one had to find a ditch or at least a shallow trench. Low sandbagged walls would have to be built around all tents and bivouacs in danger areas. The enemy was thus contriving new ways of extending the bounds of the battlefield and narrowing the zone in which we could enjoy some sense of security. We found even less reason for content as we sat round our bivouacs that evening.

On the first of September we were ready for battle. The band and some other fortunates had gone back to act as reserves, but final orders had not yet been received. Towards the late evening unexpected rumours began to travel round the camp. The attack, it was said, had been cancelled. A joyous leap of relief in my breast was almost immediately stilled by a feeling that such a miracle at the eleventh hour was impossible. When I awoke the following morning the camp was already in a state of tremendous excitement. The miracle had really happened: for once rumour had proved true. The morning light seemed to shine in a new way. We had been reprieved—and reprieved, it seemed, not from the normal toll of battle but from certain annihilation. The recent rains, we were told, had made movement on the front quite impossible and the loss of a number of tanks, which had stuck fast on their way up to the forward areas, had come as the last straw to headquarters.

We marched away towards Steenwoorde and, failing to find billets there, eventually came to rest in a camp a few kilometres from Abeele. Looking round the camp that night I saw faces that shone with smiles and heard carefree voices. Here certainly were the high spirits of the indomitable fighting troops of Britain about which newspaper reporters still wrote and talked such nonsense. Had any of them been in Abeele on that early September day in 1917 they would really have seen what they so often described, but it is certain that the reasons for the high spirits would not have been communicated to their readers. Few men, and those only exceptional men, could revel in the shadow of death, even though to most familiarity can breed a certain contempt. Those other nights had been silents nights, when men had moved mutely about as though waiting for something to happen, hoping always in their private thoughts that something would happen—accident or sickness perhaps—to liberate them from the awful prison to which our freedom had brought us.

For the next three days we wandered indecisively around Steenworde, spending one frosty night in blankets in a field just outside the village. Each night there was bombing in the neighbourhood: the raiders, droning over in relays, dropped bombs all around. We heard tales of civilian casualties and began to get impatient at being tied down. This was a new phase in the warfare, one that was to be considerably developed later. Apprehensive nights helped further to fray our nerves.

On 5th September we marched off again, in the direction of Cassel. Much to my disappointment, we climbed the hill but missed the town. While taking the regulation halt at the top the resting column was invaded by a crowd of street vendors, mostly women and girls, with baskets of chocolate, fruits and other dainties. Foolishly some of the men made purchases, which they knew to be against regulations. They were 'put on the peg' and officers and N.C.O.s—no doubt under special orders—did their best to make the rest of the march a real misery for all of us. I never minded essential discipline, but this sort of thing seemed pettifogging and lacking a sense of proportion. Though not among those singled out for punishment, I fretted at the injustice of it all. We finished up in a barn at the end of a muddy cart-track not far from the little town of Arneke. As barns went this one was comfortable enough and was to prove pleasant during the period of reprieve. The buildings were practically hidden among trees and hedges. Falling leaves were beginning to collect in the lane. There was a touch of autumn in the air.

Throughout the following week we drilled and practised over the fields during the day and went into the village at night to dine on eggs and chips. One afternoon Captain West took us into Arneke to be photographed, to provide him with a souvenir of his command, and we were touched by his consideration. Our sadness at the prospect of his departure was deepened, for we were sure we should not meet his like again. One day we were detailed to assist one of the local farmers in picking his field of beans. It was a back-breaking job for the majority of us, who were not used to field work, and I am afraid we accepted it as an alternative to drills with ill grace, since we disliked doing gratuitous work for a class whom we were sure never missed a chance of profiting at our expense.

On 12th September orders came for us to retrace our steps towards the line and two days' march brought us back to bivouacs near the village of La Clytte. Three days later we went again to the model to have explained the division's objectives in the new attack, which was to be upon the Dumbarton Lakes and Tower Hamlets Ridge. This part of the line was held by the enemy in a series of scattered concrete pillboxes, which would constitute tough centres of resistance. The attack was being planned on up-to-date lines and on a large scale. A real effort was to be made to break the deadlock on this front.

That same evening Canelle and I made an exploratory visit to La Clytte and returned in a state of reverie. About the small village there were still vestiges of the trench system of 1915 which had linked up with Locre and Kemmel, while a small cemetery near the shell-marked church contained the graves of those who fell in the early fighting, honoured warriors of a very different type of warfare.

If one of those early sufferers from the sad incompetence of our leaders could have returned to this very spot, how astonished he would certainly have been at the great transformation. The whole area of once quiet countryside was now under a continuous flow of men and vehicles and converted into a patchwork of camps and wagon-lines, store dumps and artillery shelters in great confusion. Visualising a much simpler kind of warfare, I was still, in the knowledge of the Germans' overwhelming artillery advantage in those early days, filled with admiration for those men who had managed to bring the immense machine of German militarism to a standstill in these very fields. It was thoughts such as these, a sense of gratitude to those who had come before to set us such a high example, that helped me to key myself up to avoid disgracing them. I wondered whether they could have experienced quite the fear I was feeling and decided that they could not have done. They had been trained for fighting and the machine itself had not yet achieved the inhuman proportions it had now, three years later, assumed. With memories of Jimmy Downs and Harold Eldred, visions of the Somme and Messines in my mind, I knew that should I again have the good fortune to survive there would be further scenes of horror and unspeakable mutilation stored in my memory. I would have given the world to miss what was surely coming, but I knew there was nothing I could do about it.

The next day found us in Brewery Camp on the far side of Dickebusch, 'housed' in bell tents, each of which now had its own low sandbag surround. We heard that its most recent occupants had been shelled out of the place, a report that was supported by the existence in the vicinity of a number of large shell-craters. Immediately upon arrival the Lewis-gun team was detailed to man an anti-aircraft guard. In the centre of the camp a wooden post, about six feet high, had been set up with a revolving top to facilitate the handling of the gun against attackers from the air.

We had not long to wait. Across the skies, sailing obliquely towards the camp, a regular enemy armada of planes was approaching, large bombing machines flanked by numbers of lighter scout planes. As they passed unhurriedly above I counted at least fifteen large planes, but I've no doubt there were more. The noise of the defence—somewhat indiscriminately directed,

I fear—rose to a crescendo, while the camp itself suddenly looked as though deserted. Men crammed the shallow drainage gutters which criss-crossed between the lines, or bunched down behind the low sandbag barriers of the tents. The three of us remaining near the gun with spare ammunition ready, stood up like magnified targets before the approaching enemy. Goffee fired up towards the advancing line, which was probably flying much too high for us to reach, while the Number One and I crouched near by. Even among the clatter my mind was asking why it should be me and not one of the more experienced men of the team who was taking this action. All I can think today is that this was the way I tried to minimise to myself the great weight of my fear.

Shrapnel and bullets spattered around. The marauders were directly overhead, still sailing forward with majestic unconcern. I felt a catch in my breath and my heart seemed to stand still, but no bombs fell, and for us at least the danger had passed.

But not for the camps on the near side of Dickebusch. The ground soon shook with exploding bombs and many of the camps became shambles. Now the enemy line, its task accomplished, broke and fled, each machine making a bee-line of its own to safety. As far as I saw, none was brought down.

That night the whole area was strafed by the enemy's heavies. Shells fell in the village and round the camp with nerve-racking regularity. We could hear the gun fire and gauge the arrival of the missile with certitude. It was probably a heavy piece of naval type mounted on the railway and brought up specially for the shoot. We were not sorry to leave such a hot-spot for the line on 18th September.

BATTLES OF PILCKEM RIDGE AND LANGEMARCK

The methodical artillery preparation, which had been intensified in weight and persistence by the British from campaign to campaign, reached its zenith with the Third Battle of Ypres and at this stage had, in fact, already passed the point of maximum returns. Countered by the flexible defensive methods of the Germans, who on this front supported their effective network of strong-points by a system of organized counter-attacks carried out by fresh divisions held back until the last moment out of artillery range, much of this great artillery fire-power was expended unremuneratively in soil which became more and more soggy as the campaign proceeded.

The Battle of Pilckem Ridge began on 31st July. By the end of the day, after stiff fighting, General Gough's Fifth Army had pressed forward to an average depth of three thousand yards. The ground captured included important enemy observation areas in the Gheluvelt plateau near Clapham Junction, and the rise to Bellewarde and Pilckem had been attained, but heavy German resistance and counter-attacks had prevented further progress and imposed a period of consolidation. On the right flank the Second Army's operations, which were to depend upon progress made by the Fifth Army, were confined to improving observation positions at one or two points in front of the Messines Ridge.

On the British side losses had been severe enough, again after a successful advance to the first objectives, and the ground conditions were found to be particularly exhausting. The lengthy preliminary bombardment had seriously churned up the rain-soddened ground to render progress at some points almost impossible, particularly to tanks, which suffered numerous mishaps even in attaining their jumping-off positions. On the German side, while their defensive tactics were proving effective, heavy casualties among the first-line troops were already initiating the flow of reinforcements towards the Ypres front which was to be one of the vital consequences of the campaign.

Despite these initial difficulties, Sir Douglas Haig instructed General Gough to continue with the original scheme, but only after proper consolidation of the ground already occupied and domination of the still active enemy artillery had been achieved. In any case three days of continuous rain, which had set in on 31st July, converted much of the battle area into a swamp and rendered further action immediately impossible. Even when the rain ceased on 4th August the weather continued stormy and unsettled with no sun or drying wind to clear up the mud and more rain in prospect.

The next assault, on 10th August, was concentrated on the Gheluvelt plateau, now considered the key-position which had to be gained. The aim was to advance some eight hundred yards, through a belt of strong-points, to the German second line, including the occupation of the stiff obstacles of Inverness Copse and Glencorse Wood. Against stiff enemy resistance and shocking ground conditions, this thrust was partially achieved only on the left, where Westhoeck Village was captured and the final objectives almost achieved. On the right the attack was a complete failure and the dominating positions, including the two woods, remained in German hands.

At this juncture, his reserves being all involved, General Gough had to ask for reinforcements, and the Second Army was asked to transfer three of its best divisions. To comply with this request the 47th and 14th Divisions went to II Corps on 14th and 15th August respectively and the 23rd Division to XVIII Corps on the 15th.*

The new attack, planned for 14th August, had to be postponed twenty-four hours, and heavy rain during the afternoon of the 14th, which again soaked the battle area, led to a further postponement till 16th August. In this operation, known as the Battle of Langemarck, only on the northern flank, including the town of Langemarck on the Ypres-Staden railway, were the objectives substantially achieved, assisted by the French First Army which advanced its adjoining front to the north as far as the St. Jansbeek River. Elsewhere British gains on the Gheluvelt plateau, in many cases offset by immediate German counter-attacks, were quite insubstantial. Under impossible ground conditions the attackers' losses were heavy. By the 17th of the month the battle had come to a halt, but despite everything orders were issued for a further attack on 25th. Subsequent local attacks to improve the jumping-off line for the next thrust again had little success, except on the northern flank, and the attacking troops, after heavy losses and having to

* The author's division: the transfer would have held little significance to members of the ranks, even had we known about it!

withstand fierce counter-attacks and further onsets from the elements, again had little success.

At this point of failure Sir Douglas Haig in his great disappointment decided to transfer responsibility for the main operations on the Gheluvelt plateau from General Gough to General Plumer. The new plan was to advance on a frontage of 6,800 yards between the Ypres-Comines canal and the Ypres-Roulers railway in a succession of attacks with limited objectives.

The Second Army was to take over the front of II Corps early in September, but in the meantime the Fifth Army was to continue to press the enemy. The new general offensive, fixed for 25th August, was cancelled, but minor thrusts on 27th August, in accordance with the revised policy, led to considerable further losses and very little gain in position.

The following quotation from the Official History *explains not only the end of these fated operations but also the part assigned in this battle to the author's unit and the reasons for the change of plans mentioned in the text:*

> *As the following day was also one of rain and gale, in the evening Sir Douglas Haig ordered the limitation of further operations by the Fifth Army until the Second Army was ready. An exception was made of the attack, under Fifth Army orders, by the II Corps on Gheluvelt plateau; but as the weather continued wet, that operation was cancelled on 31st [August]. The capture of the woods on this front was to be included either as preliminary to or as part of the main offensive by the Second Army, after the corps and its frontage had been transferred from the Fifth Army.*

During the August fighting on the Ypres front British casualties had amounted to 3,424 officers and 64,586 other ranks, while, according to the Official History, *the hard conditions and great discomfort had discouraged all ranks more than any other operation fought by British troops in the war. On the credit side were the effects of the great strains thrown upon the German defenders, which has been emphasised by German military authorities. One result was that the French front had been left unmolested.*

During the same period a successful thrust had been made by the British outside the Ypres area in the Loos-Lens sector to the south, which had achieved the capture of Hill 70, a vital point to the Germans, since it afforded wide observation into their lines.

CHAPTER V

BATTLE OF THE MENIN ROAD

Before we left Brewery Camp for the line a raiding party had come back with reassuring news. This small group of volunteers from the battalion had gone up to the front to carry out a probing attack over the very ground selected for the regiment's onslaught. The area had been isolated by a heavy artillery box barrage within which the raiding party had penetrated the enemy defences and returned to our positions without casualty, although later one man had been killed in the enemy's counter-bombardment while they were on their way back.

I was filled with great admiration for these volunteers. Among them I remember one man in particular, a private who acted as one of our company runners. Unmilitary in appearance and small of stature, always undemonstrative under stress, he neither gained any distinction nor accepted any rank. I do not recollect his name—though it may well have been Smith—or even remember whether he survived the war, but he was surely one of those unassuming, inherently brave men, unsung in history, upon whose presence at moments of crisis so much depends. It was only right that this group of volunteers should be left out of the forthcoming attack.

The stage was now set and no last-minute reprieve was to be expected. Everything was ready. The Lewis gunners had recently been supplied with new web equipment supporting large pouches in which spare circular Lewis gun magazines could be carried. Our ordinary small ammunition pouches had been removed from the normal equipment, which permitted the new web carrying equipment to fit over like a glove. In action this was to prove much more effective than the previous method of carrying the spare magazines in unwieldy buckets slung loosely over the shoulder.

Reveille on 18th September was at 4.30 a.m., but we were not pressed for time, for it had been arranged that the clearing up of the camp could be left to the reinforcements who were to stay with the transport. Among the latter was Corporal Goffee, whose absence we regretted, though we knew he well deserved a break on this occasion.

Leaving at 10 a.m., our daylight trek to the line enabled us to appreciate even more clearly than before the great changes that had taken place in the forward areas since the recent battles. The platoon filed out, with good intervals, along the banks of the Dickebusch Bund and across the once dead ground of the old Salient. Here was a real transformation. Everywhere, hidden behind banks and hedges, there were artillery emplacements, sandbagged dug-outs and other structures. Usually there were recently made shell-holes not far away, showing that the enemy was pretty well aware of what was going on.

Passing the serrated ruins of Ypres on our left, we entered the ancient Salient, where the process of clearing up had already rendered much of it unrecognisable, except where one passed a well-known landmark, such as Shrapnel Corner, marked by a notice-board. Here, in fact, the fumes of a heavy shell still hung about the roadway, as we negotiated the unhealthy spot as fast as our legs and loads would allow us. The low ridges, now occupied by our own troops, stood up clearly before us, and it still seemed somehow wrong to be walking there in broad daylight. A wooden roadway now led like a raised causeway across the shell-shattered ground, while duckboard tracks meandered off at intervals from left or right, bound for some destination clearly marked on wooden signposts at each junction.

Eventually we approached the ridge, where the scene of desolation challenged description. All around us stretched a morass in gradations of grey and black which looked like some petrified inferno from Dante. Waterlogged shell-holes almost touched one another, rendering the ground pretty well impassable except where the duckboards ran. Gaunt leafless trees stood out aimlessly here and there to break the monotony. Peril threatened everywhere off the tracks. Perched along the ridge itself, barely hidden from the enemy, one of our field batteries was firing furiously over the barrier, while heavy German shells were searching along the crest in reply. In the hollow lay the derelict corpses of a couple of tanks, hopelessly bogged and badly shattered. Farther over to the left were the remains of what had once been a dense wood, where shells were bursting aimlessly amidst the pathetic tree-shafts. Our guide now led us off the main road and it was clear that we were bound in the direction of the barrage. Admonished to keep good spaces, we began to penetrate the fearful wood.

The track was a narrow one, winding round filthy holes of polluted water. With every step the shelling became more intensive. The entrances to the dug-outs, for which we were making, appeared clearly in the bank ahead. But the track continued its meanderings, carefully avoiding the dangers of the earth beneath, but taking no account of the even greater dangers of the skies above. Tension rapidly increased, until human endurance could stand the strain no longer. Hunted by the bursting shells, we suddenly broke from the track and made a bee-line across the waste towards out destination. Some floundered immediately in the filth and regretted leaving the firm and narrow path. Others, more by luck than judgement, skirted the yawning pools, terror sharpening their senses. With a feeling of relief the fortunate ones literally hurled ourselves into the burrows leading into the Tor Top Saps. Among those who never arrived were a sergeant and a private who had returned to us but a few days previously after recovering from wounds. They had no need of special graves amidst those sump holes: the whole terrain was a cemetery, the slime automatically engulfing the wounded as readily as the dead.

We spent the rest of that day in the saps, learning to breathe again. After nightfall we moved forward to the line, where part of the platoon occupied a considerable two-storied strong-point.* Our Lewis-gun post was situated on the roof in a hollowed chamber open to the sky, but the position proved to be untenable under the heavy shelling and we were soon withdrawn. In the lower chamber we had an observation point through an opening, facing the enemy line, which must have recently been his

* I do not recollect the name of the strong-point, though no doubt I knew it well enough at the time. The map suggests Stirling Castle, a famous point of reference, but this seems to be just a little farther back than one would have expected, although it was directly in rear of the battalion's objectives on the morrow. If so, the awful wood I had mentioned would have been Sanctuary Wood, which on a previous occasion we had penetrated from our side of the line.

tradesman's entrance to the fort, for that is what it undoubtedly was, a massive concrete structure below ground-level, communicating with the German trench which had now been reversed into our front line.

The place was so well embedded in the earth that shells thudding into the ground above did little more than set the structure in vibration and keep our nerves on edge. The sentry at the observation point had to keep well back and out of the direct line of fire of a German sniper, whose bullets continually hit the door frame or ricochetted into the wall of the passageway outside. Fierce whirlwind strafes were undertaken by the artillery on both sides throughout the twenty-four hours. At such moments the world seemed literally to have gone mad. As a preparation for the forthcoming attack the effect of this experience can well be imagined.

In the afternoon, during a significant lull in the enemy bombardment, I gathered sufficient courage to pay a visit to the roof, to watch our artillery shelling the woods and high ground in front. The particular shells seemed to be throwing livid flails of flame which zigzagged just above the ground and I assumed that they were cutting the enemy wire for the morrow.

The morrow! My heart stood still at the thought. These last hours before a battle were always the most torturing. From the comparative safety of our fortified position the forthcoming experience assumed proportions of difficulty and horror that transcended the realms of possibility. If only some alternative were open. But I knew that I had no choice—and I could see no valid reason why I should again escape mutilation or death. All reasonable odds seemed to be against it. Fortunately I was very tired and decided that the best thing to be done was to get some sleep. Such is the resilience of youth that my invitation to Morpheus was completely accepted.

It was after dark when I awakened, with a start, to discover my comrades already adjusting their equipment. This was the moment of departure. Strangers were mingling with us, the people who were taking over the post. I envied them their sheltered position during the bombardment and began to wonder, without rhyme or reason, as one does on such occasions, why I could not lose myself among them, realising, of course, that this would merely eject me from one sort of pickle into another, that might well turn out to be little better. I knew I was just a puppet in all that was taking place and craved some way of taking the initiative. But, of course, the authorities had been giving as much careful, loving attention to the forthcoming masque of death as any showman to his puppet show.

We filed out into the trench and the fresh evening air. Both artilleries had gone silent. The night was cold and clear. An unearthly light seemed to envelop us. Surely we were in some land of make-believe! I pulled my greatcoat closely round me as, with the rest of the file, I lolled against the side of the trench, silent as the grave—waiting. An officer appeared with a jar of rum, passing from man to man along the file. I gulped down my share thankfully and felt warmer, but only for a short while. There were still too many cold hours of waiting ahead of us to render this medicine effective, but we were grateful for the gesture.

Now we moved out into No-man's-land, a stretch of flat ground little touched by shellfire. It was so devoid of features and hiding-places that neither side had wasted ammunition upon it. The heavy fire which we had been experiencing had been largely concentrated upon strong-points, whose whereabouts were well known. White tapes, which showed up clearly even in the darkness, had been laid that evening to mark the several jumping-off positions. Grass still grew in patches here and there. Hereabouts there was a wide gap between the lines, the nearest German pillboxes being some hundreds of yards away. We went well forward to take up our appointed stations, while still farther ahead were sections of 'A' Company, who were providing the front wave of the advance. At a later stage we were to pass through them, according to plan, to take secondary objectives, while later others would pass through us to the final objectives.

The Lewis-gun section had occupied a large shell-hole, which we thought would afford some shelter in case of the bombardment that seemed very probable. The night was unusually quiet, but we were not deluded that this could continue right through to the morning, although, in fact, it very nearly did. The whole area around us was teeming with movement. Why the

Germans did not smell a rat I could not imagine. A sweeping barrage across this ground could have administered fatal casualties. An occasional Very light arose from among the shadowy trees which I had previously observed. Time seemed to stand still: the cold increased. Now and again an officer came round the groups to caution and check up. Far away to the right one of our batteries fired an occasional salvo, which seemed to trickle in a most leisurely manner towards the enemy positions before bursting. But behind us and straight ahead all was still.

Suddenly an enemy battery away in front opened up. I saw the flashes of the guns and then the shell-bursts which silhouetted crouching figures between us. The bombardment continued, shells dropping all over the assembly area, so that we felt sure that our movement had been spotted. In any case this was a nerve-racking prelude to the attack, a demonstration of where the enemy barrage could be expected to fall. The firing ceased as suddenly as it had begun, and all was quiet again.

The stars began to fade, as the promise of a new day began to invade the eastern sky. Above us the heavens slowly changed to a clear blue, while out of the dusk in front the trees of the wood began to appear, their tops wreathed in morning mist. From the surrounding groups came a murmur of suppressed voices and the metallic clicking of bayonets being fixed. I pulled the straps of my ammunition panniers tighter. All was ready. It was about 5.40 a.m.—'Zero hour!'

An officer coming forward from the groups behind us snapped his watch into his pocket and signalled us forward. We were moving: a few moments silence—intensified, eternal! Then the guns crashed out from behind us and we were running forward in the reflected light of the artillery. I could feel and see crowds of men moving on all sides, spreading waves of humanity directing their puny flesh towards the enemy positions. The earth simply shook with the discharges. The air above us seemed to be roofed in with rushing shells, while some way ahead a curtain of flame and smoke completely blotted out the landscape.

We were now moving forward as fast as our feet could carry us, for we were rather farther back than we had expected and knew that comparative safety depended upon our being close to the barrage. My mind was vividly aware of the surging press of humanity. I saw our Sergeant Rhodes, who was acting company sergeant-major for the occasion, rushing among the groups, admonishing all and sundry to keep moving. Now I experienced a peculiar, almost dreamlike illusion. Though my feet were moving with all the energy needed to carry me with my burden across the ground, I felt that they were, in fact, rooted to the earth, and that it was all my surroundings that were moving of their own accord. For a brief moment I was detached from the awful present.

The noise was shattering. Dense smoke was now wreathing across the ground, causing us to gasp for breath. From out of the wall of flame and fume rose unmistakably the enemy's coloured signals of dire distress. No shells had fallen near. We seem to have been in front of the enemy's barrage, if there was one. The ground was still comparatively clear, though here and there I saw clumps of broken wire, which the advancing line, tending to bunch, was doing everything possible to avoid. So far, I had seen no one fall.

Our barrage—a wave of inconceivable confusion—began to creep away from the edge of the wood, whose trees stood out ever more clearly as the fumes gradually cleared. Now the whole situation changed as if by magic, evil magic for us! Zip-ping. Zip-ping. Snipers' bullets began their deadly work. Machine-guns, opening out ahead began to traverse methodically across our front, like flails of death crossing and recrossing as they sprayed the advancing line. I felt the tearing stream of lead swishing across as the muzzle slewed and could hardly believe I had not been hit. A man a few yards ahead slipped to the ground and lay in a heap. Sergeant Rhodes was still in front there, urging the line forward. The machine-guns cut across again and single rifle shots syncopated their steadier rattle. The defenders were resisting with deadly effect. I heard screams around me. Agony and death seemed to be cutting into the attacking lines. From the edge of the wood, now much closer, flashes from rifles and machine-guns filled the air like venomous darts. Terror now ruled my dying world!

I could distinguish our front wave clearly, for daylight was fully upon us. And if I had further capacity for fear, such fear gripped me now. The men in front were dropping to earth, whether from wounds or for cover I could not know. Men of 'B' Company were catching up and pressing through, and then they began to recoil, and even to flow back around me. It was as though the rear ranks were still being carried forward on a momentum that the front waves had lost. The prospect was awful. My mind—so clear on all that was happening around me—conjured up a picture of certain annihilation, should further advance and, certainly, should retreat prove impossible. The shadow of the Butte de Walencourt welled up in my memory. Yet while I knew so well what could happen, I did not at that moment realise how in this much wider battle the incidents on a small sector of the front might bear little relation to what was happening elsewhere. I stumbled on to a shallow pit, from which earth had been designedly shifted for some purpose, and sprawled gratefully into the low shelter of its sides, which could hardly have been more than a dozen inches high.

There I lay grovelling for the protection of its earthy cover. I soon had a companion, who got immediately to work with the shovel he was carrying. This ungainly tool in such a restricted space soon received a splintering bullet in the handle wobbling above ground. I knew I could not stay there, should not stay there, in fact, but for the moment all initiative had left me. My one desire was to hug closely to mother earth. I feared to make the leap forward that duty clearly demanded.

Movement had begun again and figures were passing on either flank. Yet bullets continued to shave overhead or to thud near the rim of the depression. A sniper clearly had the spot marked. I saw one poor devil clutch at his chest and fall away out of my sight. Another, who was already wounded, dropped into the hole, closely followed by a stretcher-bearer. My first companion now leapt forward, to fall immediately with a bullet through his leg. He crawled out of sight. Now shells began to fall not far behind: the enemy barrage was moving up. In my imagination the pincers of death were closing in upon this spot for my insignificant benefit.

I seemed to be held down indefinitely. Probably it was not more than a few minutes. There had been a halt in the forward flow, which now began again with increasing momentum. A sergeant urged on his men; detached groups passed in and out of my vision. My inaction now became intolerable. I gathered myself to rise and dash forward, hoping that the sniper had been dislodged, or had better marks for his rifle.

The battle again came within my full vision. Our barrage was well forward, no longer closely followed by masses of troops. The attackers were moving all over the place in scattered groups, taking advantage of any cover they could find. Wicked 5.9 bursts were churning up the ground behind me. Once more on my feet, towering in full view of the enemy—as it seemed to me—prudence alone urged me forward. Straight ahead there was a gradual slope to the low horizon practically free of moving men. Our advance seems to have diverged to left and right, like two streams evading an obstacle, though there was nothing now to show why this had happened. One stream was trickling leftwards to the wood, the other slightly rightwards to a prominence which looked like the parapet of a trench. The latter objective being the nearer, I promptly made for it, still on my own. The battle had certainly not slowed up while I made this assessment. Shells were bursting everywhere, bullets streamed over from different directions. Everything seemed to be chaotic. All I now wanted was to make contact.

I reached the trench and as I breasted the parapet of this German defence position my eyes fell upon a sight of horrible carnage. A splutter of bullets forced me down amidst the horror. The trench, which was little more than a wide gash in the ground, was strewn with dead and dying, British and Germans in grim equality. The very earth was spattered like a slaughter-house. Others were crawling into the shelter of this slightly protected spot. For a moment a red curtain fell before my eyes and I saw emerging through the awful mist the fixed ghastly look of a sorely wounded German whom someone had propped against the earthy wall of the trench. Those eyes looked right through me to the eternity that was clearly so close at hand.

Men were coming up singly and in groups from the rear, crossing the charnel-ditch hurriedly, sharing with me, no doubt, the feeling that this was no place to loiter in. But I had no objective now and was at a loss what to do. The men I saw were from different units. I asked a stretcher-bearer whether he knew of the whereabouts of the Northumbrians. He replied that some had passed this way, but thought that the majority were over in the wood. As I looked across the intervening ground, now being heavily strafed by enemy guns, I could discern movements about the wood and reason told me that I had deviated considerably out of course. I had to choose between crossing that hopeless expanse—an additional hazard that I had now brought upon myself—or going ahead from where I was with strangers. Duty and a wish to join my own unit made me choose the more onerous course.

Running across from shell-hole to shell-hole, with all the open country to my right, I eventually struck the wood diagonally some way in advance and was pleased to join a party of troops who had been collected near an enemy strong-point. They proved to be members of 'B' Company, who quickly put me into the picture. All the company's officers were already casualties and the group had been holding a miniature council of war on what they ought to do next. Everything was disorganised and no one seemed to be clear about our objectives. But they did know that Sergeant Rhodes, now in charge, had already gone on through the wood and obviously it was our business to catch up. In fact, the group was already dissolving by the time I had gathered all this. Alas! other details, which I pieced together during the day, made a sad picture.

Captain West lay in the wood, mortally wounded, where he had fallen at the head of the company, still pressing forward despite an earlier wound. Even amidst so much human disaster, with the impartial hand of death apparent on all sides, I felt a stab of painful sorrow at this news, mixed with a great anguish at the senseless elimination of a good, brave and truly gentle man. Second-Lieutenant Edwards, our platoon commander, had been shot dead by a German who had already given himself up at the strong-point. His gratuitous murder, made, they told me, as though it was a gesture of friendliness on the part of its perpetrator to his captors, was immediately avenged by the sergeant leading the group. The other Germans had been sent back immediately to brave the dangers of their own barrage, which seemed to intensify with every passing moment. On the roof of the concrete pillbox a sniper lay sprawled in death on the very spot to which he had climbed immediately upon the lifting of our barrage to perform his duty in picking off members of the attacking waves. The others seemed to be as harmless as sheep as soon as they had surrendered, praying no doubt that at least they might survive.

The foliage around was still alive despite the heavy fire that had been directed against the wood. Yet every bough was shattered, while the lowest branches, with some browning leaves, hung loosely over the shell-seared ground, which was broken up by the slip trenches that the Germans had constructed all over the place. Everywhere, too, there were wire and scattered enemy stores, broken branches and tumbled trunks to make movement difficult. Bullets ricocheted through the rubbish, while whirlwind bursts of enemy shells continued to stir up the undergrowth. The wood, which had been so prominent in the battle, now seemed to be endless; yet a reference to the map, on which it is marked as 'Dumbarton Wood', shows that it is not very large. As I moved forward with the group, I could not help wondering whether its cover was misleading, and whether it might not be a more evil place in battle than the open ground which had provided my earlier terrors.

Having no proper leadership, the party began to break up and wander in different directions. I soon found myself with a sergeant from one of our other companies and two or three members of different units. We seemed to be getting lost—and it has to be remembered we had no idea how far we were from the Germans or who was ahead of us. As we entered a clearing a burst of machine-gun fire forced us hastily into a short pit, already occupied by three seriously wounded men. They complained that they had been left while aid was sought and they feared they would be overlooked. The sergeant, to salve his own conscience perhaps, but against all instructions, ordered me to stay till help arrived. I protested that my Lewis-gun amunition should have first priority, but with a laconic and somewhat threatening 'You stay' he went on his way.

I could easily have disobeyed, of course, but it felt safer in the trench than wandering about the awful wood, and I had some pity for my three companions, who were out of sight and could have remained so for a long time. They were all bandaged after a fashion. Two were in a bad way, with wounds in head and back, and nothing could be done for them until they were back in the dressing-station. The other, though badly hit in the leg, had his full wits about him and was very cheerful. We talked excitedly about the attack and I found that his experience had been similar to mine. He agreed that soon after the start there had been general confusion. It was surprising that Fritz, with his stubborn marksmanship, had literally let us meander through. After the first grand rush the attacking waves had seemed to break up into groups, to be carried hither and thither by the storm. Everything at such a stage depended upon leadership. My companion was a member of a West Country regiment belonging to the division on our right, who had found himself among Northumberlands soon after the outset. I wonder what happened to him subsequently, whether he survived the war, whether, indeed, he is still alive, an ageing man, sometimes remembering the soldier he met on the very edge of the grave.

We soon grew tired of discussing the conduct of the war and I began to look round furtively for an excuse to get away. Small parties were threading their way through the wood, some carrying stretchers, but these had other objectives and refused to be deflected to my charges. Others carried loads on the new-fangled Yukon pack. German prisoners flowed back in ones and twos, eyeing askance the bursts of their own shells, but too apparently eager to get away from it all. No one wanted to tarry at this lively spot and I was wishing heartily that my irresolution had not got me into this predicament. Stragglers told me that there was a grave shortage of stretchers and many wounded everywhere waiting to be moved. To make matters worse an enemy machine-gun, apparently firing from the ridge which I could just discern through the trees, kept spraying the clearing with bullets, although I have no doubt the firing was quite indiscriminate.

My charges moaned and cursed and I wished myself well out of it. Yet I was genuinely sorry for them—putting myself in their shoes. I realised, of course, that there was really nothing to prevent my leaving them, but while such desertion would have been right in the heat of battle, I could not feel that this was any longer the position.

At length a stretcher party came up under a sergeant who

meant business. He said straight away that he was short of stretcher-bearers and suggested that I should lend a hand. I had no stomach for such a duty and pointed insistently to my ammunition, which would be needed in the line. Fortunately he saw the point and did not insist, and I left without delay lest he change his mind. I was glad to get out of sight, but immediately the loneliness returned and the uncomfortable spirit of that blasted wood bore down more closely upon me. I was filled with terror.

Fortunately for my peace of mind the edge of the trees was nearer than I expected. As I stepped out into the open my range of vision widened upon a new and very different scene. I could see the Tower Hamlets Ridge, which had been battered by the barrage, but now had a distant stillness. In the foreground, a little to my left, there was a hollow which contained two greenish muddy patches. These had been—as I was to discover later—ornamental ponds in a park, which were marked on the map as Dumbarton Lakes. One was still crossed by the damaged timbers of a rustic bridge and on the far side men were digging. They recognised and hailed me. It was a great relief to feel the possessive loneliness of the wood dropping behind me, but as I ran across the open my flight was hastened by the plopping around me of bullets from some sniper who was still at work behind the lines, although he must have been some way off, otherwise I should hardly have escaped.

Among the row of dishevelled diggers I recognised many members of the company, who passed me along to the end of the line where three members of the Lewis-gun team, including Westgarth, were glad to have an addition to their strength. The trench was already about three feet deep: when we had got down to between four and four feet six we were satisfied that this was as much shelter as we should get in view of the dampness of the soil.

This was the hour when tensions relaxed and we felt gratitude at our survival, although we knew the battle was far from over. The fighting had passed beyond the low ridge some distance ahead, but we were holding our assigned objective which lay in dead ground. Some fifty yards or so to our right there was a clump of trees which apparently masked a pillbox occupied by the remnants of one of our platoons. A piece of trench ran out of this, parallel to the wood which I had traversed and ending abruptly a few yards from where ours began. We now occupied a length of twelve feet or so which contained five of us. Farther to the left, and in the same straight line, later arrivals were to dig two further short pits, leading to a slight rise on our left flank, beyond which the rest of the company was similarly entrenched, all now under the command of Sergeant Rhodes. Casualties had been heavy, as we already knew, although there were still no doubt others who had got mixed up with strange units. Our gun team had lost Golightly, who had recently returned from leave, shot dead through the head, while another man, who had been attached for the attack, had been severely wounded. I could gather no news of Canelle.

The gently sloping ground in front leading to the Tower Hamlets Ridge, was a churned mess of shell-holes, jagged timbers and other debris. It was from the shelter of this rubbish that German snipers had begun their deadly work after the advancing groups had passed. During the day mopping-up parties, especially assigned to the task, crossed out into the waste and disposed of those Germans who had persisted in offensive action after the ground had been lost. We both admired and hated these brave men. Admired them for their persistence and bravery, hated them, illogically to some extent, for what we considered was unsportsmanlike action. Possibly they were more desperate than brave, having been taught that they would get no quarter in any case! Of course, their persistence meant that it often worked out this way, for the moppers-up would have been foolish to take any chances.

Our new line was now on the far side of the ridge. Certainly the day's advance was more than sufficient to justify the paeans of victory which we knew would fill the newspaper headlines at home. It was so easy to overlook the price paid in lives. Even we, who knew how it had all happened, were inconsistent enough to feel elated at having taken part in a military victory.

We now experienced the lull that inevitably follows the unleashing of such an attack. The shelling had died away and, except for an occasional burst of rifle-fire in the distance, all had gone quiet. The next move was being prepared. Obviously our own artillery was being moved forward, while the enemy was withdrawing his guns to prepared positions, ready for the next phase. There were trickles of movement across the battlefield, the main route passing near our trench. Carrying parties from the reserve company now paying in sweat and danger for their previous comparative immunity, R.A.M.C. teams with much to do, Royal Engineer signallers unrolling wires as they passed, groups of officers, a series of files curling towards the ridge; while there was a counter-flow of wounded, walking and on stretchers, and groups of unarmed Germans being herded back to the cages. The latter were the docile figures which we had discovered our doughty adversaries usually to be, with here and there exceptions in the guise of the Prussian type of officer, who, in fact, ludicrously matched the complete caricatures of our illustrated magazines. To them there could have been no greater indignity than to be shepherded by an ordinary British Tommy who had no respect for their traditions. One such figure I can remember still, so impossibly foolish did he look. He came by as member of an otherwise co-operative file under the charge of a nonchalant infantryman. The Prussian, complete with pickelhaub and top boots, had obviously been passing the limit with his capers and now his guard kept the tip of his bayonet near the seat of his trousers, ready to goad him at the least sign of lagging on his part. The German, with his chest drawn high and his exaggerated gait, like that of a turkey-cock, looked so comic and incredibly unreal in that setting that a roar of laughter rose from the trench. Our enemy's face was livid and in his eyes was a look of undying hatred that boded ill for the future. I laughed with the rest, for anything that released the tensions of our position was welcome, but I did not much like the implications of the ridiculous display.

That night passed quietly, but it was damp and cold in our ditch. We were unsettled in spirit and did not know what to expect next. Counter-attack or relief—either was possible. We were hungry, for our rations had given out; consequently we were bad-tempered. The enemy still made no sign. Why was something not being done on our side? What were we waiting for? Surely this was the time to bring up fresh troops and push home the advantage we had gained? Why leave Fritz breathing-space to consolidate his new positions? What was the staff doing? Probably they were still in bed filled with pride over the success of their plans! Thus we talked and argued among ourselves, for want of anything better to do. We were ignorant, and no doubt unreasonable. We hoped that whatever did happen we should miss the next move. Perhaps, on the other hand, we were not unreasonable in our surmisings? Our leaders seemed to hover between overconfidence and inability to profit from complete success. Perhaps we were right in feeling that the lack of action now was tantamount to failure. There had been a feeling after the battle that there was no resistance ahead. We had gained this impression, although we were no longer in close contact. The upheaval in which we had been involved had just petered out. The enemy's barrier of steel and concrete had been pierced, or rather smashed open by our artillery and occupied by our puny selves. Something should now be done to exploit his weakness. This is how we felt at the time, but what we did not realise is that 'military science', which had shown both sides how to create such situations, had as yet not discovered how to exploit them. The vast military machine was too ponderous to become mobile again at the vital moment. And so we waited.

The surrounding quiet and our bad humour continued on the morning of the second day (21st September). We had no continuous line and it was necessary to send runners between the fire-pits. This movement did not seem to matter in that dead spot, and, in fact, others, without any special need, got out to stroll about out of sheer boredom. The more cautious of us—perhaps the better trained militarily—attempted to discourage this, but without success. Shortage of N.C.O.s increased a tendency to indiscipline, and there were those among us who had had no previous battle experience. I remember one man in particular who took a foolish delight in running backwards and forwards to talk to cronies. In reply to our protests he sneered at us for being 'windy'. This indeed we were, and cautious, too. At the time it was not thought we were under observation, but one could never be sure. Later in the morning the doubt was settled when an enemy observation balloon appeared just above the horizon far ahead of us, but our restless colleagues still refused to listen to our advice. The day wore tediously on.

It was, I should think, about half past three in the afternoon when the silence was at last broken by an enemy shell which burst near a strong-point just behind us on the edge of the wood. This was occupied by a Vickers-gun team. Thus began a bombardment which the enemy kept up steadily for the next four hours. The late enemy pillboxes suffered heavily. We hoped that our position, unmarked on the maps, would get off lightly, but we were soon disillusioned, with a burst right on the edge of the trench. Crash! Crash! Crash! These were funny shells which seemed to take fire and slice along the ground like scythes, reminding me of the wire-cutting bombardment I had witnessed from our strong-point just before the battle. The Germans no doubt thought we had gone to the trouble of putting up wire, and possibly had interpreted our desultory movements in this way. We cowered down in the trench while the terrifying wave of destruction passed within a few inches of our heads. One of the early victims was the foolhardy cat-on-hot-bricks of the morning. He was badly hit and whimpered like a child, as a stretcher-bearer braved the storm by running from a neighbouring pit to bind up his wounds. For once I felt no pity, for I considered him as largely responsible for what was now happening to us. Hour after hour this terrible shelling continued, with methodical certainty. Each shell seemed to be making straight for us: each time terror mounted to breaking-point within me. There was a blinding flash and a rush of air as the muck shot over us: again and again the shell burst on the edge of the trench. Surely the next one would do the trick? Thus awaiting death, a frenzy of fear seemed to take hold of us and we cowered further into our burrow, not daring to show a finger above ground. Yet, despite the accuracy of the fire and the law of averages, we escaped. By the end of the ordeal the trench was literally lined along both edges by shell-holes. Neighbouring pits had not been so fortunate. From time to time we could hear the cries of the wounded above the din.

Night was beginning to fall when, just after the bursting of an enemy salvo, the haggard figure of Sergeant Rhodes appeared through the smoke, shouting an order to retire one at a time to the wood. Here was something tangible at last. We could move and get away from this particular target. Nothing could have been more intolerable than to have to continue under the slow bombardment: movement would break the tension.

The first man clambered out of the pit and ran towards the wood. The rest of us straightway lost both patience and control, and followed suit. In panic I rushed towards the remains of the rustic bridge which lay directly in my path. The screaming of the next salvo was already in my ears as, bending almost double, I crossed the swaying planks. One of the shells burst in the mud of the pond, throwing up a shower of filth, as I ran blindly on and stumbled into the wood. This seemed now to be literally filled with men sheltering behind the tree-trunks. I saw the shapes of numerous steel helmets where their owners lay amidst the undergrowth. I threw myself down and settled behind a low bulge made by the roots of a large tree.

In front, not more than forty yards from where I lay, a Vickers gun which had now been positioned on top of the German strong-point was pumping bullets in a rising trajectory over the ridge ahead. It was nearly dark, but the light from the enemy batteries and the shell-bursts on this side made the ridge stand out as clearly as before. The flashes of our own guns from the rear lit up the silvery tree-trunks weirdly in the surrounding inferno. Orders were shouted that an attack was to be expected and that we should be ready to resist. A low rattle of withdrawn bolts came from the surrounding banks.

The enemy barrage now seemed to lift and fall with full force upon the wood. Out in front a red light shot low, fell over the ridge and burnt itself out on the ground, suffusing the waste of shell-holes with a pale crimson glow. Other lights followed and our guns redoubled in intensity as they replied to the SOS call. The enemy was attacking all along the line.

The wood now was in a terrible upheaval. From above, spiteful shrapnel shells burst downwards, spattering the branches with bullets, while high explosives burst below, causing here and there a tree or large branch to fall with a crash. I took out my entrenching tool to scrape away the mould and improve the cover at the foot of the tree behind which I lay. A direct hit would have been the end as far as I was concerned, but this was the smaller hazard in such a wood, which really afforded poor cover from such an onslaught. We had hardly improved our chances by leaving the trench, but no doubt the move had been ordered as part of a general scheme of defence. Thus I clutched my rifle, expecting every minute to be my last. A form a few paces away leapt up convulsively and fell back with a scream into the gloom. Death was stalking to a grim harvest through that wood. On all sides I could hear cries and groans and could only marvel that anyone survived.

The shells were now falling so quickly that the aisles behind were filled with dense fumes. I tried to stuff my ears against the horrible din. Lying next to me just out of reach I had recognised a member of No. 5 Platoon. He was now burying his face in the mould and showing no movement, yet I did not think he had been hit. The stress of action in coming to the wood had overcome him and for the time being he seemed oblivious of the inferno by which he was surrounded.

From the direction of the line a continuous crackle of musketry now came through the din. The attack was developing. I gripped my rifle more tightly. What should we do if Fritz broke through? He would come down over the ridge and attack the wood. We hadn't a lot of ammunition, but anything would be better than this infernal shelling.

Over on our left front the sky became red with flame, as though a wave of fire was pouring over the edge of the world towards us. This was the final touch to an unbelievable scene. Nothing like it had I ever experienced, for this was something that was not merely visual: I felt myself caught up in an integral part of the holocaust. Evidently the division on our left was recoiling before the liquid fire attack, the flames of which now reflected luridly across the vale between. I could no longer believe the evidence of my eyes, or my senses. It was all too incredible. It seems foolish now but I thought of white beds—beautiful white beds—and nightmares! It would soon be bedtime at home. Some shrapnel spattered into the mould not far from my head. A struggle was going on within me between intense fear and mental exhaustion. The battle continued. Men screamed in the throes of death—and still I was not hit.

At length the enemy shelling seemed to slacken and a change came over the situation. No more shrapnel shells burst overhead. The red glow in the sky faded away, while the noise of rifle-fire out in front subsided to a desultory splutter. Only the German heavies continued their strafe, while our Vickers continued its non-stop racket. A runner came out of the darkness on his way to headquarters. The enemy attack had failed. Our barrage had been too much for them: from all the noise it must have been pretty deadly. The runner passed on into the wood to complete his dangerous mission.

A little later a file of men began to pass forward, at wide intervals and bending low to avoid the flying shrapnel. A relief was on its way to the line. This thin line continued to trickle by. Enemy shelling had definitely slackened. Some of us got to our feet and walked over to the the strong-point, where we joined in conversation, discussing the prospects of relief. For a moment caution was relaxed and we forgot our danger. The sudden whine of a missile, unmistakably directed, and I threw myself headlong under a sandbagged lean-to, where six or seven others were already sheltering. The shell burst with a blinding flash but a few yards away. It must have blown all in the opposite direction, for I saw no one hit. I was a few yards away when the next one came and I had no time to take cover. Standing bolt upright, I saw it burst right on top of the strong-point where the machine-gun was placed. The whole crew was blown to smithereens into the darkness, the explosion immediately stopping the rasping rattle and momentarily converting that corner of the wood to silence. Their survival for so long in such an exposed position had been little short of miraculous. The gunners had surely earned a decoration; now they would merely be posted missing. My own astonishing escape from the shrapnel and blast so near at hand I was long past considering.

A little while later further parties moved across the scene and a N.C.O. shouted that our relief was in. I did not question this order. Still half-dazed I followed a moving file back into the wood, proceeding along a path among the trees. Shells were still falling around, but none very close. At the outset I knew there were men behind me. Then we came to a branching of the path and there was a good deal of argument. Shells burst nearby and some of the file took shelter in shell-holes. I followed those moving ahead of me and soon became aware that I was at the very tail of the file. I hailed the man in front, discovered that he was a battalion runner and realised that I was with the wrong party. We left the wood, came to a well-defined corner where there were the remains of a dump, consisting of nondescript boxes, barbed wire and pickets. A party of officers and orderlies, coming in the opposite direction, stopped to inquire the way. I gathered that we were bound for battalion headquarters and, realising that this was not my proper destination, in my indecision I let the party get ahead. They disappeared into the gloom and I was alone.

Alone out there in the dead ground between the lines, I was panic-stricken. Why had I not kept them in sight? I shouted frantically, hopelessly, and heard the strangeness of my voice as it echoed faintly over towards the trees. And then, much to my surprise, a voice hailed me in reply. In the shadows of a bank pierced by a short strip of road I saw two men and an empty stretcher. I was overjoyed. Companionship then meant so much. One could go mad alone in the open on a night like that.

These two stretcher-bearers had also lost their way in the darkness and had sought shelter where they could wait till the morning. The sunken road extended for no more than thirty to forty yards between banks about six feet high, but seemed to be as good shelter as we were likely to find. After comparing experiences, we decided to seek sleep under the protection of the bank. The night was now so pleasantly quiet that I found no difficulty in dozing off. I woke with a start. Something had happened, but I was too bemused to figure out the situation, until a shell burst at the end of the road. We were again under bombardment. My companions woke up. We decided that we should be as safe where we were as anywhere. It was very cold. I took out my entrenching tool and began to hollow out a funk-hole in the bank. The earth was soft and crumbled easily. I was not doing much good, but the action occupied my mind and I felt warmer. The shelling had intensified: there were heavy bursts all over the area. I did not know how near some of them had been. After so much previous stress I seemed to have fallen into a dream, wondering just what was the truth. If Fritz really was shelling, he surely knew just where this short cutting lay. At any moment he would just drop a shell right into the gap, and . . .

I heard it coming straight for me. A tearing explosion and the bank toppled over, a blanket of filthy earth came down upon me. I was pinioned to the elbows. Only my legs were free and these I was kicking feebly. I could get no leverage and my strength was going. Earth filled my eyes, my ears, was getting into my mouth. I could not breathe. My brain remained clear. Fritz, I thought, had got me at last, and it was not really surprising. Then I felt a tugging at my feet and my companions pulled me free. Had I been alone I could not have survived. Now I was dazed. Blood streamed down my nose from a slight cut on the bridge. This was my only actual 'wound'. I cleared the earth from my ears and spat out the filthy soil.

The other two hustled me away. There was a trench quite near, they said. We ran and soon came to a belt of wire where we were challenged as we slipped through a gap and into the trench. My companions disappeared, as though they did not want to be spotted and I never saw them again. But the strafe was continuing and the occupants of the trench were obviously more intent upon getting shelter under the parapet than interrogating strangers. A shell fell very near. I saw the narrow opening of a sort of funk-hole among the sandbags and slipped in. There was little room. Someone cowered in the other corner. 'Who's that?' he asked. 'A stranger; you've no right here. Get out.' Then I saw sergeant's stripes on the man's arm. I was frightened enough, but this N.C.O. was literally crying with fear. I cursed him and told him I was staying. I could understand his fear, a thing none of us could control on occasion, but I regarded him as a low sort of swine to want me out in the storm. The truth was, he was ashamed at being seen as he was. He cowered in his corner moaning. I had no business there. He would have me arrested. A shell dropped at the back in a cross trench branching away from the main trench and the smoke curled in through the opening, nearly choking us. He kept quiet after that.

When at last the bombardment ceased it was getting light and they were shouting 'Stand to' along the line. Thinking that the infuriated sergeant might trump up some charge which I, a stranger, might find difficulty in countering, I slipped back into the trench and lost my identity among the motley unkempt defenders who lined the trench. I saw the woods in front appearing through the morning mists and adjudged that I was back somewhere in our original jumping-off line. An officer came along collecting particulars of strangers and I was surprised to discover that something like half the men were from different regiments. At this very moment a party passed along in front among them I recognized Weatherall and other members of the company; I hastened to join them. We soon reached a support trench which had been assigned to the company for assembly. This afforded respectable cover and was well supplied with dug-outs.

I was hailed by members of the platoon who cheerfully told me that they had thought I had 'snuffed it', as they put it. Many had been missing after the bombardment in the wood. The most astonishing case was that of our stretcher-bearer, 'Kidder Delicate', who shortly after our withdrawal to the wood had been seen literally to disappear in a shell-burst. He had been reported blown to pieces and his death was very much regretted, for he was highly esteemed for his ministrations to the wounded. However, back here he had been found fast asleep in a dug-out, which was reminiscent of a similar incident in Battle Wood.* He had little to say about his miraculous escape! I discovered that the relief had come in, as I had gathered, but that owing to confusion in the dark most of the company had spent the night in the wood. I had really got farther then the majority. Soon after our arrival food was issued and I suddenly realised that I was ravenous. Then I went straight off to sleep in one of the dug-outs.

It was some hours before I awoke. During the afternoon our position was heavily strafed, but the dug-outs were deep and we suffered no further casualties. Needless to relate, we were in a very jumpy state later, when we were withdrawing along the duckboard track. There was a general bombardment in progress from both sides, but it happened that our route was not a particular target, so that nothing fell near. On the way we ran alongside a moving file of an Australian battalion, also on their way out. These tall, proud men in their fine quality and generously tailored uniforms had always inspired in me a respect tinged with envy, for it was well known that the troops from the old British colonies were all treated much better than we were,

* See p. 71 above.

just as we were generally better paid and equipped than our European allies. On this occasion it was all different. I found it difficult to recognise in this ragged, limping, furtive and dirty-looking column our normal Antipodean comrades. 'Say, Tommy,' uttered a husky voice, charged with an emotion it is hardly possible to convey, 'this is Hell.' A grunt of approval passed down the two files as we drew apart to our separate destinations.

We spent the night in bivouacs at Bedford House hard by Ypres and marched the following morning to Brewery Camp. During a halt on the way we found ourselves near a canteen, which those of us who had money straightaway raided. Only one or two were quick enough to get served before the officer in charge of the party, immaculate in his clean uniform, for he had been one of those detailed to stay behind, ordered us out and made us pass the remaining minutes of the halt sitting on our packs in the roadway. We were stung by the pernickety injustice of this procedure, feeling that army regulations could very well be forgotten once in a while for the survivors of such an ordeal as we had just been through. We groused all the way back to camp.

During the afternoon there was a bathing parade. With all the dirt of battle thus being cleansed away I felt in the seventh heaven of comfort and anticipation of a real night's rest. So many times had I now come through a major battle unscathed—or practically so, for my small wound was already healed—that according to the law of averages my future could be assessed as hopeless. At that hour, however, with the latest of the ordeals so close, it was hardly necessary to bother about the immediate future!

Our company's casualties had been heavy, totalling about half, including all the three officers who had taken part. Number 6 Platoon had lost fourteen members, besides our leader, Mr. Edwards. Among those killed was a Corporal Ball, with whom Canelle and I had consorted on the little stream at Serques. Incidentally, he had been one of those who had the good fortune to be left out of the Messines attack. Of Canelle I still could obtain no news and the best I could now hope for was that he had been wounded. The battalion had taken a number of prisoners.

TO THE END OF THE YPRES OFFENSIVE

Despite the disappointing results of the opening battles of the Third Ypres campaign, Sir Douglas Haig adhered to the view that the situation elsewhere, particularly on the French and Russian battlefronts, rendered the continuance of British pressures absolutely essential. At a meeting of the War Cabinet early in September he had to counter strong proposals that British resources on the Western Front should be strictly conserved during the remainder of 1917, as well as to withstand pressures to send aid to Italy, where General Cadorna, the Chief of the Italian General Staff, wished to step up his attacks upon the Austrians. Nevertheless Haig maintained his point, even though he had to impose a halt of three weeks in the operations while stocks of certain howitzer shells were being built up. Among his many worries the prospect of further bad weather and an overall shortage of reinforcements were insistent. In the event of the Ypres offensive coming to a standstill, plans were worked out in some detail for operations on other sectors of the front. Not that Haig was without his supporters, for as late as 19th September, when further action was imminent, he received a request for a renewal of pressure from General Pétain, who appeared to regard the situation on the French front as pessimistically as ever.

The new attack was to be concentrated on the Gheluvelt plateau and, while the general plan remained unaltered, the tactical scheme was radically revised. The full weight of the Second Army was to be massed against the plateau, the occupation of which was to be carried out by a succession of assaults or 'steps', as they were called, with strictly limited objectives. At the same time the Fifth Army, now assuming a secondary role, was to press forward in the north across the Steenbeck valley. The artillery was to concentrate on selected targets, while the infantry were to be given specific tasks in clearing the ground of the enemy as the line went forward. Special attention was being given to the renewal and clearance of the roads and tracks leading into the battle area.

The initial stage, to be known as the Battle of the Menin Road, was fixed for 20th September, the first of a series of thrusts at six-day intervals. Zero hour was at 5.50 a.m. The main attack was delivered by four divisions from right to left: the 41st; the 23rd; the 1st Australian; and the 2nd Australian, with supporting attacks on the southern flank by 39th and 19th Divisions and to the north by units of the Fifth Army. Three sunny weeks had hardened the ground and the new methods of attack proved highly successful. Divisional objectives were attained, except on the Tower Hamlets Ridge to the right, and immediate German counter-attacks were frustrated.

The Official History *refers to the 23rd Division as follows:*

> *In the sector of the 23rd Division, the left division of the X Corps, a single strong-point in Dumbarton Wood (just west of the lakes) caused heavy casualties to the 68th Brigade.* But despite this temporary check and the difficulty of keeping direction in the dense smoke and dust raised by the artillery barrage, the first objective beyond the marshy ground north of Dumbarton Lakes was reached a few minutes after the barrage and a defence consolidated along the upper reach of the Bassevillebeek. The 69th Brigade, faced at once by the remains of Inverness Copse, was able to penetrate the litter of wire and debris without great difficulty; small parties of Germans, however, who remained hidden in covered shell-holes till the leading infantry had passed, opened fire on the battalions moving up behind, in artillery formation, ready to leap-frog to the subsequent objectives, and inflicted severe losses on them. Sixty Germans who resisted in this manner were killed by the moppers-up. Beyond the first objective a line of dug-outs north of Kantinje Cabaret on the Menin road gave trouble and groups of Germans in them, about forty in all, only surrendered after a tough struggle, in which the brigade trench mortars took a prominent part. These dug-outs were taken by the 9th Green Howards, whose success is the more praiseworthy as they had lost heavily in passing through Inverness Copse. Eight of the sixteen company officers including two company commanders, having been killed or wounded.†*

* * *

> *On the arrival of the 23rd Division and 1st and 2nd Australian Divisions along the second objective about 7.45 a.m. a fresh breeze from the south-west rolled away the mist, and the value of the morning's achievement was apparent. The sight which met the eye brought that thrill of victory always hoped for but so seldom experienced in previous offensives. The strongly defended neck of the plateau between the Bassevillebeek and the Hanebeek re-entrants which had defied all the August assaults*

* All the company commanders of the 11th Northumberland Fusiliers became casualties. The opening barrage had fallen beyond this stronghold.

† See *Official History.*

had been forced, and the 23rd Division by its capture of the Kantinje Cabaret area was firmly established at the root of the Tower Hamlets spur. Inverness Copse, with its bitter memories, was left behind. Ahead in the clear morning sunlight the two Australian divisions could see across the brown wilderness of shell-holes and shattered tree-stumps to the farthest limits of the plateau about Broodseinde; and by the capture of Anzac House they had removed the chief German artillery observation post overlooking the Steenbeck valley to the north.

The Official History *refers to local attempts by the Germans to improve their positions, but no specific reference is made to the German counter-attack of the afternoon and evening of 21st September described in the text. During the period 20th to 25th September, covering this particular battle, the Second and Fifth Armies sustained a total of 20,255 casualties.*

* * *

By this time the 11th Northumberland Fusiliers were in no condition to take a leading part in any major operation, and although the battalion was to be involved in the two subsidiary, but none the less agonising, incidents described in the following chapter it may perhaps be convenient to summarise the rest of the campaign at this point.

The next step was planned for the 26th September, with its main object the capture of Polygon Wood, which was to give its name to the battle. Despite a well-organised German spoiling counter-attack in the early morning of 25th September between the Menin road and Polygon Wood, which met with only slight success, the new assault went ahead substantially as planned and with satisfactory results. Stiff German counter-attacks were all frustrated. They were defending key-positions! Losses on both sides must have been equally heavy.

The following step on 4th October, known as the Battle of Broodseinde, met with equal success and it was clear that the new British methods of attack were paying off. In fact, reports at the end of the first day indicated that the enemy had received an overwhelming blow from which recovery would not be easy. The number of prisoners taken was proportionately higher than usual, as was the number of German dead on the ground. Messages stressed the demoralised state of the survivors.

But now the inevitable break in the weather came. After a fine period the rains began again and army commanders immediately felt that the campaign should be closed down. Sir Douglas Haig, however, for many reasons, not the least of which no doubt was exasperation of letting victory slip when it seemed so close at hand, decided to continue.

Despite deteriorating conditions, the next assault was fixed for 9th October. This, the Battle of Poelcapelle, was a failure. The story of the summer was being repeated. Men who could fight men were unable to overcome the elements. Even now it was decided to persist until the higher ground around Passchendaele had been reached.

In the first Battle of Passchendaele, launched on 12th October, both the second and the Fifth Armies participated. The advance achieved was limited and casualties high. A further thrust was held up until 26th October, pending an improvement in the weather. This Second Battle of Passchendaele consisted of a series of thrusts on 26th October, 30th October, 6th November and 10th November, in which Passchendaele itself was captured by the Canadians. Although a part of the main ridge to the north still remained in German hands, the time to call a halt had surely come; many would say it was long overdue.

Sir Douglas Haig gave the word on 20th November. Events elsewhere were contributing to this decision. British casualties on the front during the period 31st July to 10th November have been officially stated as 244,897. German figures are not available but there is sufficient evidence to indicate that they were just as high. The Official History *suggests they may be as high as 400,000, although one would not have expected the losses of the defenders to have exceeded those of the attackers, whose number we know, was unusually high.*

So ended a famous battle. Whether the slogging match was justified remains a question of high controversy that can never have a final answer. Yet, however one may assess the folly of men in high places who allowed such a situation to arise, one thing at least can be said: from the evidence that survives no one who took an active part in the operations had reason to be ashamed of the company he kept.

CHAPTER VI

PASSCHENDAELE

On 24th September we marched back to a training camp in rural surroundings near Westoutre, with hope in our hearts, and for a few days the late summer sun shone down upon the golden foliage of that pleasant countryside. The contrast between hell and heaven could not have been more absolute. In our gladness at survival and present felicity the blank places in our ranks soon came to be overlooked.

Yet I was sadly grieved on the following morning when I heard officially that Canelle's body had been found on the Tower Hamlets Ridge on another battalion's front. His cultured manner, such a contrast in that rugged company, lives in my mind over the years. A gentleman in all senses of the word had been squandered on that September day and the world rendered so much poorer. Self-consciously and with heavy heart I fulfilled my promise to write to his home. How superficial must have appeared my poor sentences of regret telling of something that I had only learned at second hand! I was not surprised, therefore, to receive a very curt reply from my friend's sister, a disdainfully worded heart-aching letter, asking for further information, which I passed to the new platoon officer for his proper attention.

The battalion paraded before General Babbington, who delivered a laudatory speech on its contribution, which I believe was justly worded. The blank left by Captain West was filled by a Captain Sterling, transferred from 'C' Company. He was a tall, efficient-looking type, whose kindness was masked pretty effectively by a stern demeanour. He was, I was told, a solicitor by profession and his reputation with his former company did not suggest that he would easily replace his much-beloved predecessor. That he eventually did so and indeed shared a similar fate does not fall within the scope of the present narrative.

Other gaps in our ranks were filled in a much less acceptable way. The battalion was joined by a draft of some two hundred 'other ranks' who had just been combed out as fit men from the Army Service Corps, Royal Horse Artillery and other service and transport branches, which we usually regarded as specially privileged. Naturally they were not well pleased at having been switched to the P.B.I.* Among them there were a number of Mons men, while the majority had crossed the water by 1915. Few of them had yet been under fire, but this deficiency, in our eyes, was far outweighed in theirs by their long service in branches which had their own prestige. We knew they would take some assimilating, but what was to prove the biggest blow was the discovery that they were all sweating on leave and would automatically go to the head of the list. Faint hopes had already begun to dawn in my mind of going home in the not too distant future, but such hopes were now completely dashed. In fact I was not to get home on leave until after the Armistice, more than a year ahead.

I could not realise at the time that this was but an example of the way modifications in an individual's prospects are frequently brought about in public services by official changes in policy that are beyond his personal control. As a civil servant I was eventually to have similar hopes dashed, or at least delayed or curtailed, by similar policy changes on the part of authority. The lesson that in mass society the individual and his personal contributions are of small import was, of course, clear enough to me at the time, for the impact of consequences we consider unfair is too real to be argued away, but I was then foolish enough to imagine that this was one of those peculiarities of army life to which I was only temporarily subjected.

Westoutre was a pleasant village with many attractions. It was out of bounds, but passes were easily obtained. One evening, accompanied by Wilkinson, a quiet, music-loving hairdresser, I went there in search of eggs and chips, a dish which, as I've already remarked, was always a great standby with members of the ranks. My relationship with Wilkinson was always friendly, for I discovered that he was a much more interesting conversationalist than most of my comrades. Nevertheless our friendship never developed, partly because he was a type who tended to

* 'P.B.I.' was short for Poor Bloody Infantry, a term widely used by the other branches of the army at the time.

take over specialist duties, but at this period in particular I had come to consider myself something of a Job, and not a very fortunate sparring partner. One evening I went to Westoutre to see a show by 'The Dumps', our quite excellent Divisional Concert Party. They were giving a nightly show of the revue type, popular at that time, a continuous song-and-dance entertainment in which a mixture of bawdy and pointed allusions to our betters combined to keep the audience literally doubled up with laughter. Had we been students of psychology, I feel sure we should have seen this entertainment as an excellent means to releasing those tensions by which we were all inevitably troubled. Others presumably went to the town in search of sexual release, and I have no doubt there were adequate facilities at hand, though I do not remember that this was a matter that came prominently into my mind at this stage.

Our quiet spell was to be little more than an interlude. On the evening of 27th September disquieting, and in fact unexpected, rumours got about the camp that we were returning to the line. The following morning we transferred to huts in a wood near Groote Vierstraat, where we were to be in reserve for working parties. The wood lay back from the Messines Ridge, and at its northern edge were situated crumbling defence works which had been used by our troops during the early months of the war.

The night was disturbed by the droning of enemy planes flying low overhead. As the wood camouflaged our position, we did not get up, although bombs were being dropped all around. Nevertheless, the close approach of a plane seemed to make it certain that we were not to be overlooked! The experience was therefore nerve-racking. The war of nerves, hitherto intermittent and ineffective, was certainly being stepped up by the Germans, and no doubt also by ourselves!

On the following afternoon I was detailed for a working party which still lives vividly in my memory. By this time the heavy batteries had been pushed forward and the service areas were encroaching steadily upon the old battlegrounds of the Salient and Messines. Work was in full progress in these areas in broad daylight. That afternoon we tramped forward like a slowly curling snake amidst the throbbing activity, past heavy batteries only slightly camouflaged, in hectic action against the enemy. Our path sometimes passed right through the battery area, even under the muzzle of the guns which were tipped skywards. If they were in action we ignored the fact, each man keeping his own counsel as the file trickled forward. This was always an ordeal to me, who in my childhood had been susceptible to loud and sudden bangs, a nervous reaction I had never completely mastered. On this occasion I managed to move forward steadily until the last few paces, when I broke into a run, fearful lest my companions should see that I had the wind up and a little reassured when I noticed that others were doing likewise. Occasionally this precaution was of no avail: the gun fired just as I drew opposite. There was a vivid flash as the heavy missile thundered skywards, followed by a rush of air that caused me to catch my breath and sway like a leaf in the wind. Then I became steady again and all seemed well until the path began to curl towards another battery and I set to wondering how near we should approach this time. Great was my relief when it became evident that we should pass to the rear of the guns.

Every trip to the line was an adventure fraught with new and unexpected perils. Always my mind was in a turmoil of nervous expectations, few of which materialised as anticipated, although in the horrific circumstances of the Salient the worst fears rarely transcended reality. This particular afternoon shells were falling here and there, sometimes in the distance on the horizon itself, sometimes not far away. Would the track avoid the danger spots? Would the shelling continue until it reached the edge of the distant wood, whither we appeared to be bound? Or would Fritz suddenly alter his range to bring this section of the track within his target? And if he did where should we turn for cover? Such were the thoughts that jostled through a mind insufficiently distracted from the terrors of the moment.

Here and there in the lee of a stunted hedge, and usually masked by a low bank, we passed the low sandbagged shelters in which the gunners, engineers, pioneers and others spent their days when not actually occupied. We did not envy them their billets in such a place, though it was obvious that their job was less dangerous than ours. Yet one wondered how they managed to survive for long stretches. Some, of course, did not; the war of attrition went on all the time. An unexpected shell-burst, and a body up to that moment full of life and vitality drops to the ground a broken mess: there is need for another of those simple wooden crosses, of which the pioneers maintain a good supply.

As we proceeded in the late September sunshine a flight of enemy planes crossed our route, sweeping steadily nearer, despite the myriad of shell-bursts by which their progress was being contested. Plop! Plop! Plop! Our anti-aircraft shells burst in the sky around the marauders, who sailed apparently oblivious of the hail of steel wasting itself in the vast depths around them. We wondered where our own planes were, grumbling that they were never around when needed. I watched with a mixture of fascination and terror, fearing the worst. It was time for a halt, and as we rested we saw the bombers dropping their cargo across the path some way behind us. Obviously they had been in search of a much more worthwhile target than an insignificant file of infantrymen!

We reached the shattered terrain that had once invested our front line and had now become the area of the field guns. Just here we passed a string of small guns standing, apparently derelict, in the semi-morass. In fact, they were carrying out a slow shoot with their servers under maximum cover. At regular intervals a man ran from a dug-out opening, pushed a shell into a breech, discharged the gun, and ran quickly back to shelter. This was the only time I was in a position to see such a manoeuvre and I felt that the battery commander was to be congratulated for thus ensuring the maximum of cover for his men.

From a dump in Sanctuary Wood we drew boxes of bombs which were needed in the line. The track, leading upwards away from the wood, continued in the lee of a low ridge, whose slopes were covered with broken tree-stumps. For the moment all was quiet and we felt we could well rest a while, for the job was burdensome. As I sat on the edge of the track I could look back over a wide stretch of country across the hollow in which the wood lay. A more desolate and depressing sight would have been difficult to imagine. The black waterlogged earth was constantly churned up by the shelling, which went on intermittently, but with deadly effect, day and night. Everywhere there was muck and rubbish, the debris of war and the flotsam of the armies, from an empty bully-beef tin to the pink, rotting, half-engulfed carcase of a mule. And from it all came a horrible stench of war and death, the nauseating stink of churned-up cemeteries mixed with high explosive.

As we rested we became aware of peculiar shells bursting by a roadway across the wood, four or five hundred yards away. As each shell landed a sheet of flame squirted round like a fountain. Our interest was particularly drawn by these incendiaries. especially when one clearly hit something. A fire sprang up and then seemed to die away amid a black shroud of smoke which billowed along the ground. Antlike figures of men began running but in different directions, as though there was some sort of panic. Stretching farther along the road we could see clearly piles and piles of ammunition boxes. Suddenly the white line of the dump disappeared in a vast sheet of flame—a miniature Messines, which seemed to lift a black mass into the heavens. Even at our distance we had to crouch down in shell-holes to avoid the rain of burnt wood and metal that seemed to well like a wave up the valley and to fall around us a few seconds later. When the smoke had cleared the dump had been replaced by a line of charred debris.

Many in the vicinity must have met sudden, horrible death. But such a happening was not to cause our mission to deviate in any way. We continued along a winding path, past Stirling Castle, the vast German strong-point which was probably the one in which we had assembled before the recent attack, across a second depression to a low ridge unenviably occupied by a battery of field guns, ending up at Clapham Junction, where we deposited our bombs.

For a few moments we loitered to look at the ruins of the German defence system, among which a dismantled miniature artillery piece of the pom-pom type particularly drew our attention. It appeared to have been sited in the enemy trench for anti-tank work, and the derelict tanks which now decorated the sullen landscape behind us suggested that it may have had its successes, although in truth the very nature of the ground would have been sufficient to prevent these premature monsters from piercing the German defences. They must have been veritable death traps for their crews. At a corner, where the trench lines seemed to knit together, a board had been placed warning all who approached that the spot was under enemy observation, although it may by this time have become out of date. Through a break in the skyline one could see beyond the ridge across a wide stretch of rolling country, much of which must still have been in enemy hands. It was like a glimpse of the promised land. All around us were signs of recent and constant whirlwind bombardment, while there beyond, so near and yet so far, stretched the open country towards which all our attacks had been directed. Was victory still possible before the end of the year?

Our sergeant warned us to keep off the skyline, and without further ceremony we commenced the trek back, feeling that the worst was over. But that eventful afternoon had not yet shown its full hand.

All the time shells had been falling somewhere within our field of vision, but far enough away not to cause more than the normal degree of apprehension. On our way now to the track below the battery we saw that something more terrorising was about to unfold. Heavy shells were crashing not only on to the ridge but over into the wood to burst on either side of the track. There was no cover among those leechlike holes of dirty water: we had to keep on. We ran through the danger area while the shells continued to burst in the waste, throwing up fountains of slime. Above us the ridge was literally ablaze with fire. I had rarely seen such a concentrated bombardment, and it is quite possible that the shells which were falling about the track were also intended for the ridge. I saw one burst right in a gun-pit, throwing the wheels of the gun into the air as though it was a disintegrated toy cannon. Its neighbour had already been overturned, while the few shelters dug into the ridge were giving up their occupants, who were scuttling down the bank like rabbits. As I ran, breathlessly but fortunately unburdened, it seemed that the shells were concentrating upon me as in a nightmare, but they pitched shorter and shorter as I left the danger zone behind. I halted to take breath as our last man came running through the awful wood. Shells, still pounding the ridge, seemed to be changing its very contours as the black earth sprayed and billowed under their terrific blast. The gunners must have suffered grievously. We had one serious casualty and waited while he was brought along. After a weary walk we reached camp at 7 p.m. without further incident.

That night there was a good deal of activity in the vicinity, both by our artillery and enemy planes. There were rumours of heavy casualties from the bombing, but, except that the next morning the wood was saturated with the smell of gas, we seem to have occupied an island of quiet amidst the surrounding turmoil. It was Sunday, which meant church parades and a day of rest until the evening at 6 p.m., when we again left on working party to the line.

Naturally we were filled with apprehensions. The Germans had been using their new incendiaries to good effect. On the way we passed by a heavy battery whose heavy rag camouflage had caught alight and was burning fiercely. The gunners, flitting like gnomes against the flames, were straining every nerve to keep the blaze away from the stacked ammunition. After the brightness, the darkness was intensified and it happened at the same time that artillery activity had ceased on both sides. It was like walking in the quietness after a storm, except that we knew that the surrounding shadows were pregnant with danger.

From Observatory Point we carried water up to Clapham Junction and returned. It remained quiet. There was something uncanny about it all. The front that night was not itself. As we waited in a trench while our officer went for instructions we noted that near-by trenches seemed to be crowded with silent Tommies, waiting motionless as though oppressed by the darkness. It seemed that an attack of some sort was expected, which we on our part devoutly hoped would be delayed until we had got away. We did, in fact, get away and as far as I know nothing happened. The stillness had been terrible and we were all oppressed by it. It was such a night as we should in all reason have welcomed, with not even a chance of casualties, and yet, so much did our imaginations make cowards of us, I feel sure that we would have been relieved if some warlike activity had occurred to break the unnatural quiet of the front. Even the frogs seemed to be subduing their chorus!

The next morning, the first of October, brought an unexpected but very welcome surprise. Lorries came to take us back into the country. It was not usual at that time to transport the infantry in this way, except in emergency, and we all appreciated the gesture. It happened, too, that our journey was full of interest taking us along the road that ran parallel with the Messines Ridge and affording extensive views of the battlefield. This inspired a good deal of discussion as we went along, the old hands in particular searching back into their memories. In any case the infantry, so intimate in the detail of battlefields, rarely had a chance to see things in wide perspective and this was for us a special occasion. The ground behind the ridge, sloping up gently to the horizon, was still criss-crossed by trenches and belts of broken wire, and littered here and there with the usual debris of battle. It was a bleak, ill-begotten terrain not yet under the clearing hands of the Royal Engineers, while far up the slope heavy fountain bursts of large German shells indicated clearly that the tide of battle had not gone far beyond the ridge. We were bowling along at a carefree speed on the very edge of the war, passing, in the foreground at the roadside, a continuous fringe of abandoned dug-outs and old rubbish-bogged shell-holes. We passed by the famed hill of Kemmel, pointing prominently into the sky, through Locre and Bailleul, names made famous by the regular divisions in 1914 and 1915, who to us had become almost as mythical as the Gods of Homer. Bailleul was still a thriving market town with its thronged ancient square containing many well-filled shops and an imposing Mairie. Our destination proved to be a camp of bell-tents, which we pitched ourselves, just outside the large village of Meteren, still a pleasant rural place, despite the presence of a variety of army units. Here we stayed a couple of nights.

In the large Y.M.C.A. a concert party, styling themselves 'The A.B.C.s' were giving a show of the revue type to which we flocked for joyous relief. The company, we thought, was a mixed one, although at first I had had my doubts, for it was strange to find so many Englishwomen in the battle zone. The actual performance immediately stilled such doubts, for the females of the troupe were so essentially feminine and had such dulcet voices that any idea of impersonation seemed out of the question. Could they be nurses from a not far distant hospital? It was a delightful entertainment which long before the conclusion had the entire audience in an ecstasy of collective emotion.

No doubt a much less competent show would have had its failings masked by that upsurge of amorous feeling. Great was the shock therefore, and unrestrained the immediate laughter, when at the finale the wigs were removed to disclose the all-masculine truth. Even greater was the generous applause which marked with appreciation, not unmixed with disappointment, the effectiveness of the subterfuge! That night bombs were dropped in the area: later reports from a neighbouring battalion mentioned many killed and wounded.

Walking just outside the village among the green fields I saw a number of black-lined crosses which marked the graves of Uhlans killed there in an early skirmish during 1914. Now, in October 1917, the countryside was so settled and peaceful, behind the bastion of trench lines dividing it from the enemy, that it was almost impossible to visualise those early days when the German advance guards pushed on so far with practically no opposition. Swaggering and confident, journeying on beautiful horses in the manner of the medieval knights through a peaceful summer countryside; some of those German cavalrymen had met an Allied patrol and had thus paid for their impetuosity. Swagger and horses, even nature herself, had since been blotted out by the new manner of warfare which those Uhlans had not lived long enough even to visualise. The new days of trenches and high explosives left no place for flamboyant chivalry! Thus I mused at the sight of those lone crosses, overcome as always by the enormity of death coming to young men in health such as myself. The idea was incredible, as though the advent of death in such a setting were irrelevant, despite all evidence to the contrary. How much more incredulous would I have been on that October day had someone told me that within a matter of months the Germans would return in force to these very fields and overrun many of the quiet rural places which I had learned to regard as completely protected, at least from ground attack.

Our battalion came to rest again in Le Thieushouk, not in the field of bell-tents now abandoned because of the air-raids, but in a barn a little way down the road. Our parades were carried out in the large meadow behind the barn. Captain Sterling, in course of discovering his new command, had us drawn up for inspection in full marching order. He was not satisfied. The consequent ill temper of an earlier sergeant-major, who had only recently rejoined us, fully confirmed the sour reputation of that objectionable individual. He was a hateful person and, although sergeant-majors were notorious for this sort of thing, I do not remember anyone in the army who made himself so universally disliked and in such a short time.

We were also drilled by the second-in-command of the company, Lieutenant Hewitt, an ex-Guardsman whom we saw only rarely on account of his absences at the Brigade School. Spare, dapper, well-groomed, Hewitt was the traditional officer of the old school: a splendid word of command, he strutted the parade ground like a turkey-cock, partly by skill but even more by sheer force of personality and example, making us drill at least a hundred per cent better than normally, so that we were surprised at ourselves. Strangely enough we enjoyed the ordeal, for ordeal it was, appreciating the discovery that mere amateur soldiers could be made to do the impossible. Hewitt, despite his habitual absence from the trenches, was greatly respected. He was the type that, on the parade ground, would tolerate not the least incorrect flicker of an eyebrow, yet off parade was friendly without being condescending, an attitude which so many of his amateur colleagues would have done well to emulate, though in truth many of them had not got it in them.

One evening on my way back from Caestre I was shaken out of a pleasant reverie by the bursting of a heavy shrapnel shell above the road about fifty yards ahead. Another illusion was thus shattered in that quiet countryside. My loneliness was intensified. I shook with fright and I was again glad that there was no witness of my quite disproportionate show of fear. There had been a significant change in these back-areas since the spring, and I did not like the prospect. Both sides were busy learning how to wage a war of nerves. This, of course, had been British policy from the beginning, with the constant war of attrition in the trenches, by means of raids and the like, even when there was nothing much to be immediately gained. Now the sphere of such tactics was being widened. It would become more and more difficult to get away from it all during our rest periods.

Our rural interlude was unexpectedly shortened. It was on the evening of the 5th October—I was preparing my belt for a stroll—when I became aware of a commotion outside the billet. The orderly sergeant was issuing orders to bystanders that we were to pack and be ready to move to the line at once. It was then 7 p.m. Runners were sent round to the estaminets and soon the whole company was rounded up. Rations were issued and we were ready to move off by 8 p.m., surely a record for such an unexpected move. Motor lorries rushed us to Ypres and we were soon moving out of the town through the Menin Gate.

The Menin road, creeping away into the night, seemed to symbolise the endless road to eternity. Out there in the darkness it surely led on for ever. On either side in the gloom one could just discern the broken ground, an incoherent mass of disused trenches, abandoned battle rubbish, and dim crosses, warning us not to deviate from the beaten track, which in its turn was anything but healthy territory.

That night the scene from the road was so typical of that phase of the war as to remain engraved upon my memory. Flashes from batteries hidden out in the broken ground constantly split the darkness. A regular stream of transport flowed away towards the bursting Very lights, moving aside ever and anon to avoid a shell crater in the road itself. Just outside the town we passed the stinking bodies of dead mules, thrust aside to keep the way clear. Pools of blood still marked the place where the poor beasts had fallen, although some hours had probably passed since they had died, for their ripped-up carcasses were already adding vigorously to that stench of disintegration to which one never got used. I literally reeled as the smell assailed my nostrils and did my utmost to hold my breath until we were out of range. There were other corpses around, already swollen to gigantic proportions and from which ghoulish rat-forms scurried as we passed. Unburied human bodies, sons and husbands of quiet folks at home, also lay with the dead animals. Thus in single file through this hell we continued to creep along the road, keeping well to the edge so as not to impede the progress of the transport.

Shells burst at intervals, here and there not far from the road. Fritz was in no hurry. He knew that a shell on that crowded target was bound to hit something, and there was plenty of time. That shelling was leisurely and nerve-shredding. And now and then, as if stirred up by this desultory action, the stink of dead mule welled up out of the darkness. We went forward: we halted and waited; and then went forward again. Frustration intensified in our souls, for we began to realise that we were going nowhere and at such a time and place there could have been no worse destination. Indecision had taken control. We murmured and we cursed; we almost cried in our aggravation. Then we were turned about and led back into Ypres, cursing even more roundly such futile leadership.

Back in the city of ghosts, we wandered among the shadowy pediments that had once been fine commercial buildings, and at last found a billet in a large cellar. The floor was of stone, and cold: stars shone through the gaps in the 'ceiling,' which was actually the original ground floor, supported by a number of metal pillars, some of which had been knocked out of position. In the morning light the cellar looked even less secure than it had felt in the darkness! Bacon and tea were served from a field-kitchen and orders to move were received immediately. At the last moment I had to go in search of a latrine, built among the broken walls at the rear of our underground billet. It was well constructed, showing that the cellars had been much used as billets, but this I imagine had been during an earlier period, since much more cover would have been desirable in Ypres at this time. It was a good thing I was in a hurry, for the Germans chose that moment to commence a brisk if not very concentrated morning strafe. As I rushed off towards the parade, which was assembled in the derelict street outside, a shell fell in an adjacent cellar throwing up a fountain of rubble.

We were being transferred to the Infantry Barracks, where we stayed a few hours. This was the only occasion I visited this well-known peacetime building, which had been used by our troops in the early days as a defensive position against the German flood. It was a massive building with walls many feet thick which still presented an effective breastwork against enemy fire. Here and there, it is true, the outer walls had been breached, but in the main the shells had done little more than chip into their well-knit courses. This was certainly surprising in view of the extent of the onslaught. The Barracks still stood up, a massive bulwark amidst the shattered buildings in that part of the city. We were led down into a corridor in the lower part of the building, which had been fitted up with netted bunks still affording a reasonably safe refuge amidst the turmoil. A small central court showed many traces of the bombardment, but the walls on the far side still held firm. During our brief stay shells did hit the building without inconveniencing us. The masonry of that antiquated fortress could evidently put up a good defence against the onslaught of modern artillery. Down in that basement we were delighted to find a canteen, but our hopes were immediately dashed when the man in charge told us there was nothing to be had, though he was optimistically expecting fresh supplies at any time.

Later in the morning a party of a hundred of us was chosen to go forward again. We set off with little enthusiasm, quite in the dark as to what was expected of us. We were soon out on the Menin road once more, but now in the rain, which reduced visibility and caused the entire countryside under the loaded skies to look like an endless waterlogged marsh, as indeed to a large extent it was. We kept to tracks running in parallel to the road and eventually reached somewhat higher ground where the little village of Hooge had once stood. This, we knew, had been one of the famous battlegrounds of the early days of the war. Had it not been for the splintered notice-board at the roadside, I would not have had the least suspicion that the few insignificant heaps of powdered bricks were the remains of a once thriving Flemish village. The road here crept over a ridge, the landscape on either slope of which was absolutely bare. In a hollow over to our left, where the road branched, we looked down on to a large dressing-station which lay hidden from direct enemy observation.

When we arrived, however, the place was a scene of frantic activity, indicating that the area was subject to constant bombardment. Indeed, a barrage had been sweeping the ridge even as we approached across the broken ground and had only just desisted. It was between such waves of terror that the R.A.M.C. men had to get going. At the entrance to the station, which led down into the bowels of the earth, a number of loaded stretchers awaited attention while others were being hurried across the open to a waiting ambulance whose driver was sitting intently at the wheel ready, and obviously eager, to get away with his human freight as soon as authority should say 'go'. More carriers were arriving as our party threaded its way into the area of activity; a continuous stream of wounded of both nations was trickling in. In the middle of the hollow among the group of workers I noticed a slight figure of a man moving purposefully among the stretchers. He wore a dirty green uniform, clearly emblazoned with a red cross, a German officer. Our R.A.M.C. guides told us that he was a doctor, captured some time before, who had resisted all efforts to send him back. They spoke with awe of his skill, asserting that he knew more about the work than all the rest of them put together, and that he was rendering inestimable service in the very difficult conditions. I looked at him with respect mixed with wonder. The call of humanity no doubt transcended any feelings of enmity he may have harboured, and, of course, he was helping his own men as well as ours, but I still found it difficult to understand the weight of devotion that caused anyone to stay in such a place when he had the undoubted right to go back to safety. He moved about as though impervious to all thought of danger and I wonder now whether he survived, as I hope he did.

Mumbling warnings not to tarry, our guides hastened us up the slope to a dug-out opening alongside the track and down a flight of steps which pierced steeply into a passage dug-out that no doubt eventually joined up with the dressing-station itself. It was crowded with R.A.M.C. men, stretcher cases and walking wounded, so that we had a job to find a place within. The reason for the hustle was not long in doubt: hardly had we gained this earthy cover than the furies again broke loose over Hooge. The earth trembled: muck and fumes billowing down the stairway indicated how close to the opening the shells were falling.

We were now made fully aware of our mission, for mission it was. We were to go forward to fetch wounded from the front line, where cases had been building up tragically and communications had almost been annihilated by the enemy bombardment. The fearful tales of our R.A.M.C. companions, who were clearly rattled, the infernal racket above, the memories of a similar errand of mercy at Eaucourt l'Abbaye on the Somme, composed a picture in my mind that made me sick in anticipation. I wished that I might assume the cowardly gift of invisibility and retreat to some quiet limbo unseen by my companions. I almost prayed for the courage to run away. But I realised from experience that the only cure for my sad condition was the thing I most feared—the order to do something rather than to squat there waiting for it.

We were, in fact, waiting for empty stretchers. The call upon them had been so great that the current batch of wounded had to be dealt with in the station before we could be equipped for our mission. At the same time carrying parties were being knocked out and casualties collected at the dressing-station were mounting continuously. We waited what seemed quite a time, listening apprehensively to the storm without. I even began to hope against hope that there were no more cases to be fetched! Eventually, however, a small supply of stretchers became available and I was one of the party nearer the opening which was detailed to go forward.

At the moment there was a lull in the strafing, although the fumes and smell of high explosive still wreathed across the ground from which we had now issued. We pressed forward quickly, feeling instinctively that as there was little cover in the vicinity the farther we got away from the dug-out the better. Nevertheless, we had hardly got fifty yards before a salvo fell venomously across the path ahead of us. One of our party dropped automatically like a log. We thought he had been hit, but he had just fallen senseless at the concussion and, as we heard later, he was carried back to the dug-out with loss of memory and thus for the time being automatically protected from further strain! A second man was severely shell-shocked; he reeled back towards the sap like one pleasantly tipsy, quite incapable of controlling his reactions. These were the first bad cases of shell-shock I had seen since the Somme and were still as incomprehensible to me. However frightened I might be—and this was my normal state—I never felt like this. My only lapse, on Hill 60 during the Battle of Messines,* had, or so I thought, been caused by actual *force majeure*. My attitude was still one of disbelief. I felt that this reaction was one of inferiority that ought to be controlled. I was sorry that human beings should react in this way, but despised rather than pitied the actual victims who gave way to such

* See p. 64 above.

weakness. One must remember in retrospect that this sort of thing was then completely new to one's experience.

We hurried forward, striving to get quickly out of the zone of immediate terror, and were quickly entering the advanced battle area, a horror of slime and shattered trunks which one could feel as well as see around one, a condition of things that ate into one's consciousness, so that only a genius in art or word could have conveyed to the uninitiated the real horror of it all. Ever and anon the track we were following passed between solid blocks of concrete which had once formed enemy pillboxes, now shattered, although there were others that were practically intact. Here and there in the watery morass lay the hulks of our tanks, in various stages of disablement, lurching foolishly into the mud. The picture was completed by the short jagged stumps of Glencorse Wood sticking up out of the mud like questioning fingers. It was now drizzling and we were thoroughly soaked—a minor evil, offset by the advantages of having a damp cloak of invisibility draped across the battered land.

We came to the region of current struggle on the Passchendaele* front. All the tracks were littered with the dead, in muddy brown and dingy grey, while here and there the dissolving vestiges of some poor mortal's life-blood gave the only shuddering colour to a uniformly drab scene—apart, that is to say, from the occasional greenish-yellow splashes of mustard gas, which were hardly less horrible. We had attained higher ground, for I realised that the battlefield was now spread out before us. Over to our left was a high mound about which shells were thickly falling. Beyond this obstacle, as well as ahead of us, where there was no apparent obstruction, the ground stretched away featurelessly across deserted terrain that looked both treacherous and swampy. So much could one see and so much could one feel. Any prominent objects were obscured by the drizzle, but it seemed more than likely that we were already under direct enemy observation. Our trenches were now near at hand, while the enemy positions could be anywhere beyond. We saw at once that our mission would have to be carried out in the open, and that we should have to take what came.

* In fact, the first official Battle of Passchendaele was still some days ahead—on 12th October.

Except for the hollow rattle of a rifle bullet across the waste, it was quiet in our immediate vicinity. There were a few cases, including a sorely wounded German, ranged in the lee of a ditch. The first stretchers were soon prepared for the homeward trek. A party of eight, of whom I was a member, was detailed to go farther. Our guide led us down the edge of a muddy field, bordered by a low bank which afforded us some cover, to a broken wall at the far side which adjoined an ex-enemy strong-point. Our case had been deposited there for shelter and we had to climb over a heap of rubble to reach him. The place was very exposed: a wide landscape lay before us, much of which must have still been in enemy hands. Our own supports, we knew, were near by, but there was not the smallest movement to be discerned within our field of vision. It seems possible now that Fritz comprehended our true mission and was being indulgent for once. Otherwise I cannot see how we escaped. Even so, a sniper began to pot away at something in our direction and his bullets droned over, but either we could not have been the target or his marksmanship was unbelievably poor. Nevertheless, we felt no reassurance at the time. At any moment a machine-gun might have opened up to settle our account. Consequently we could not breathe freely until we had hurried our man across the exposed field and over the rise away from observation.

Once back upon the wooden road progress was really rapid. With eight men, four of whom were always ready to take over the burden, it was possible to proceed almost without slowing down. All seemed to be going well when the very worst happened. The Germans began to shell the track in front of us. At a bend ahead, where the road swung away in the lee of a hill, shells had begun to fall at regular short intervals, and it was towards this spot that our hurried steps were inexorably carrying us. There was no alternative, no shelter: the ground sloped upwards to the ridge, downwards into the hollow on our right. On either flank it was too treacherous to permit a detour. Our only route lay ahead on the road. Most of the shells screamed into the waste, throwing up fountains of dirt and doing little damage. But one had just hit its mark, tossing into the air the heavy baulks of timber from which the road was constructed, just as though they were no more than driftwood on a rough sea. I was now carrying, moving forward at a fair trot, for our case was too far from consciousness to be bothered by the intensified vibration as we stepped over the uneven planks. Another hundred yards and we should be out of the danger zone.

A shell had just exploded with a roar and I was breathless with fear. I was aware of the cross-slats of the roadway, passing under my feet like a Venetian blind moving endlessly, while I literally crushed my shoulder up into the stretcher. We swayed as we skirted a large jagged gash in the planks and perilously cut the bend of the road in our effort to shorten the shortest line between two points. The road now led straight ahead, downhill to the dressing-station. Another shell screamed over. I held my breath, the impossibility of submitting to the normal inclination to bend earthwards heightening the strain. The shell burst behind us, and we knew that the immediate danger had passed. It was safe to stop and wipe away the sweat from our brows, and to release the burden to our companions, who had wisely hastened ahead to get clear of the zone of fire. We soon reached Hooge and our poor devil was rushed into the sap for urgent attention. May he have survived that ordeal which had already involved unknowable terrors long before we arrived on the scene!

For a short while our immediate movements were in doubt, and we were not sorry when we received instruction to report to the dressing-station at Bedford House, where we spent two uncomfortable nights in draughty lorries awaiting recall to the line. During our first night, which I spent for most of the time walking up and down the lines to keep warm, the enemy continued to strafe the whole area heavily. Orders eventually came for us to return to the huts at Westoutre and great was my delight on our first night to be sitting in a village shop before a dish of egg and chips. I noted in my diary that on the 7th October summer time had ended—this was an innovation at that time—adding my approbation of the idea and wondering whether it would be continued in the days of peace.

On the following morning an incident occurred which, despite its small importance amidst the turmoil of those days, I was always to remember and can still clearly see, as if it had happened yesterday. We were being drilled by our unpopular company sergeant-major. He stood out in the open field bawling orders, as sergeant-majors did and probably still do, while we without enthusiasm mechanically obeyed. A poor apologetic scrap of a dog slunk miserably across the erstwhile parade ground, lurching towards the instructor as though half-consciously drawn towards that isolated pole of human magnetism. A foot jabbed out viciously and the trust-betrayed dog ran yelping out of sight, while the entire company shuddered with anger. There was no officer present.

Later that day we heard with failing hearts—for the battalion was weary and depressed—that we had another turn in the line to face before divisional relief came. During the two following days we reapproached the awful land by way of Reninghelst and Brewery Camp at Dickebusch.

The afternoon of 11th October found us back in the Bund, occupying one of the largest dug-outs and pleasurably conscious of our safety there from artillery fire. On the way in we had again passed close by the Railway Dug-outs where the military cemetery was still being constantly desecrated by enemy fire and the smell of death was indescribable.*

It was cold in that dug-out, but we made a fire at one end from a number of those beautifully constructed ammunition boxes which scroungers brought in from the neighbourhood. The smoke from the brazier filled the interior and threatened to stifle us, but what was that so long as we had a warm bed! It was certainly a comfort not likely to be repeated on subsequent nights. That night at least I slept like a log.

The scene over the flats from the Bund towards Ypres was not very different from the bustling picture we had witnessed on the eve of the Messines battle—not very different superficially but changed in the essence of things. On that earlier occasion the bustle had all been improvised: everything had just arrived or was arriving. Now the landscape was settled with camps and well-established batteries. The line was well beyond the horizon in all directions; the Salient was no more except in our minds. Today a battery of long-muzzled six-inch naval guns had taken

* I was to remember this vividly after the war when I went unsuccessfully in search of Eldred's grave, as at the time he had been reported as buried there; it is not surprising that his name was later to appear upon the Menin Gate Memorial as one of those without a grave.

up their positions before the Bund, their firing over the dug-outs removing any element of tranquility that may have previously lingered in that strange place. As we sat thinking about our beloved ones and ruminating upon the probability of early mutilation or death, news came that we were to take over on the Passchendaele Ridge for a few days from a battalion that had been badly handled in a recent attack. We all knew it was a hot-shop up there: those of us who had gone forward on the recent carrying party also knew the sort of clammy horror that the waterlogged front had in store for us.

The guide arrived on the second afternoon, the bags of rations and water-cans were distributed to the sections and we left the Bund in single file on a trek that was destined to take much longer than we then expected. On the wooden road a heavy strafe caught us in the open and we were lucky to suffer only two casualties. One was severely wounded, the other another case of shell-shock. The latter I remember very well. He was a lance-corporal who, during my early months with the company, had frequently acted as orderly corporal. In this office he had often delivered the mail, an ever-popular service and one which brought him much in contact with me, since I was the private with probably the largest incoming mail in the company. I had been dependent therefore on his ministrations in meeting my omnivorous attempt to keep up with events in the wider world. I forget his name. It is entered in my notes as Cole, but I feel that this is merely a pseudonym. He was one of our small band of regulars, a Mons man, a smart soldier and in every way an estimable person. I had missed him for a period and recently he had reappeared looking fit and well, much fitter certainly than most of us, with nothing in his demeanour to hint at the threat that obviously hung over him. Previous cases that I had seen, and have mentioned, had been anonymous to me, and although shocking enough in all senses none had had the impact of this incident which involved someone I knew and respected. It just did not make sense. I heard that this was his second relapse. It could, of course, have the advantage of releasing him from any further adventures in the firing line, although even that could not have been certain, in view of how much still lay ahead. It was always a sore temptation to the medical authorities, who had to make up a quota of fighting men, to fill in gaps with the names of those who seemed to any layman fit enough for the job. The shelling accompanied our slow progress along the track, and in the wisps of fume that shot up from the embattled muck I more than once imagined the outlines of that gesticulating figure!

As we moved forward darkness began to enshroud us and lights to suggest the closeness of enemy positions. The guide was becoming undecided. We halted in the shadow of a large mound, in which I recognised the landmark that had been pointed out the other day. Our officers took counsel and it was not long before we knew that we were lost. The prospects of a night out there without cover, cold and forsaken, intensified the fear already gripping us. An unmistakable wave of anger passed along the straggled line, and we cursed the guide as the bloodiest fool that had ever been born.

The lights that went up beyond the mound seemed to intensify the shadows of that massive uprising, but these were constantly pierced and torn by the intermittent shellfire that swept in waves about us. We scattered, we grovelled on the clammy earth, and to our frightened souls was added the terror of shapes in the darkness. How that night passed I cannot clearly remember. For periods I slept in a heap, huddled to the sodden ground, a chilled hypnotic sleep disturbed by the innumerable outbursts of shelling which no longer seemed to matter. At these hectic periods the earth around blazed like a scene from the infernal regions, but in between were interspersed blanks of blackness when I seemed to lose consciousness.

As the first dim light of day began to appear over the horizon I got up, just how and why I do not know. I was stiff with cold. My reaction had been automatic. Someone was talking. The guides had returned from a reconnaissance and were now ready to take us in. Understandably the men in the line were waiting with some impatience. Their extra spell had come at the end of a terrible experience* and their anger must have been as great as ours. Even as we moved off the surrounding landscape began to emerge and our eyes became accustomed to an utter desolation which we had hitherto only sensed in its complete starkness.

* The First Battle of Passchendaele had begun the previous day, away to the left of this position.

Very shortly we came to a rise and saw before us a large enemy concrete strong-point, which was to be our company head-quarters. Just over the rise in front was the line.

There were no communication trenches. We had to cross the narrow intervening zone in full view of the enemy. The men in the line, seeing that the eagerly awaited relief had at last arrived, at once began to stream across to meet us. It was already broad daylight. An enemy machine-gun began to traverse across the front as we ran towards the trench. Fortunately the shooting was not very accurate; possibly the perspective was misleading in that light: at any rate, the bullets flew above our heads. We reached the trench. The relief was in. The artillery was already opening up from both sides. In the comparative shelter of the trench I pitied the retiring company in their flight to safety. Our guides had much to answer for.

The front-line trench, but recently the scene of fierce battle, was dug into the saturated earth without defence works of any kind. We were stationed in a detached piece, shaped like an 'L', on the extreme right of the position, which was just large enough to contain the gun team and one rifle section. There was no below-the-surface access to the rest of the line, which curved forward from our left flank out of our range of vision. Straight ahead we could see nothing. There heaped-up earth cut off our observation and incidentally, as we were to discover, acted as something of a shield against fire from that direction. Over to the right, facing the forward-jutting arm of the trench, we looked across a swampy area which was still in enemy hands, for what it was worth, and ate back into our line. It was our job to command any approach across the waste, in which the enemy was said to have scattered strong-points. Behind us, below the ridge, there was another strip of marshy ground, a swampy valley cutting us off from the remains of Polygon Wood. This had been the obstacle that had held us up in the darkness.

It seemed little short of a miracle that our troops had been able to wrest such a position from the enemy. On the morning of our arrival the ground behind us was still littered with the un-buried corpses of friend and foe. In this nightmarish scene—one repeated a thousand times in that senseless war—we saw in terror an awful preview of our own personal doom.

The enemy's position was not known. The machine-gun bullets that had marked our arrival probably came from a post out in the swamps which lay somewhat below us.

As we had passed the strong-point in the rear of the position orders had been given for all ration bags to be deposited there. The sergeant-major was having his last bawling fling before he went to earth! It was evident that many of the bags had been lost on the way, which was hardly surprising in view of what had happened. One of our party of nine in the cul-de-sac had managed to smuggle in a jar of rum. He argued that had he dumped it at company headquarters it would almost certainly have been collared for the officers. Clearly our need was greater than theirs. The squat earthenware jar was hidden away in case of search, but it made frequent trips into the light of day. I took a tot and felt much better, although I must admit that I never needed much to take effect. The jar continued in movement and the party for moderation was very much a minority. We argued that the supply should be nursed for some more serious emergency during our spell, but while this counsel was accepted universally in theory it was completely ignored in practice. Seeing the precious liquid quickly disappearing, I took a second tot. It was not long before the emptied jar was discarded over the parados among the other rubbish. Rarely had I seen a party in such a woeful situation so joyfully carefree. Even I had lost all fear and would happily have taken part in an operation against the enemy. There was at least one hectic moment when I contemplated undertaking an offensive on my own account! But our stores of Dutch courage soon ran out and we were all cast back into the depths of dejection.

We squatted listlessly on the trench bottom, waiting for something to happen. Muck from the trench sides trickled from my steel helmet down my greatcoat. Behind me a man was relieving himself in disgusting proximity. The cold, that had for a brief spell been driven out, gradually reasserted its grip and my hands became too numb to enter brief notes in my pocketbook.

The night eventually came, and two more long endless days were passed in that trench. Artillery activity was almost continuous on both sides, invariably rising to a crescendo with stand-to at nightfall and stand-down at day-break, at which times the black earth churned over our heads like the foam of an evil sea. More rum came up with the rations and we were served with good tots. The devoted carrying party lightened our lot by getting the rations through. We could have been worse off than in our cul-de-sac, and certainly would have been had the weather turned wet, for we had no shelter.

Our chief discomfort, apart from the cold, was the restriction of seating space on the bottom of the trench, which got into an increasingly filthy state. As the shells burst casualties were mounting up. One had hit a party in front of the company dug-out. Though here again our isolation was a boon. Even though we were constantly in enfilade due to the trench's shape and some shells burst uncomfortably near, the one burst that could have settled all our accounts failed to take place, a sizzling dud. There was something unusually strange and abrupt about some of the shell-bursts, and rumour had it that these were being fired from British guns captured by the Germans from the Russians on their Eastern Front!

Officers visited us at night, and even during the day, when the trip across the open was hazardous in the extreme. On the second morning our platoon officer dropped suddenly among us with an order to open fire upon moving figures out in the waste. We could not see anything and indeed were loth to draw fire unnecessarily. Consequently, by the time the gun was aligned in the right direction even the officer agreed that there was no target. During the afternoon of the following day our hearts were lightened with the news that we should be relieved at stand-to. When later we heard that the reliefs were actually on their way, we thanked God and prayed that their arrival would not be as delayed as ours had been. Then followed one of the most frightening and, in some ways, most surprising episodes that my memories of the front still retain with abnormal vividness; yet in the reports the incident could hardly have figured as more than a normal routine relief from a somewhat hot shop.

Tension had mounted long before the time of stand-to, and when we heard that our guides had so effectively left nothing to chance as to bring up the relief while the light was still strong our gratitude was strongly tempered with apprehension lest their presence should be spotted by the enemy. To make matters worse an enemy plane droned over, unmistakably looking for suspicious movements. The almost hovering aviator began to tap out a message in Morse. A chill ran down my spine as we stood in the trench fully accoutred to depart. Events now took charge of men and we seemed no longer to have any volition of our own. Some urgent extraneous will seemed to assume control.

As a line of khaki figures appeared along the horizon from the rear pandemonium seemed to be let loose. Coloured lights dropped from the plane, while from over the edge in front fearful red rockets shot up into the sky. The relief was in, but the enemy no doubt thought that another attack was developing. 'Clear out' and 'Every man for himself' were shouted along the line. Panic took command. In a mad stampede we passed through the relieving company. Undoubtedly we had lost our nerve. What happened to our officers I do not know. I did not see one during our withdrawal, though that was hardly surprising in the mêlée.

Machine-guns swept from over the ridge behind us. The enemy barrage dropped around us in all its fury. Burdened with my magazine pouches and weakened by fatigue, I kept up with a small party feeling its way towards a clump of broken trees. We were making instinctively for a spot which promised some sort of protection, feeling doubly naked out in the shelterless waste. We were crossing the still clearly defined race-course of Reutel when the enemy plane, having fulfilled its primary mission, swooped down and raked us with machine-gun bullets. These spanged ominously into the mud around us, but no one was hit. We were a difficult target with the sighting aids then available to the airman, but from our point of view the effect was devastating. Terror and fatigue combined almost to prevent my levering myself up from the ground to which I had sprawled, but I made a great effort and continued with my companions farther into the wood. Here we found a well-defined track, along which we rushed like madmen, throwing all discipline to the wind. Water and mud spurted up all around as shell-bursts successively followed each warning shriek.

Some of my companions in their terror attempted to cram themselves into a large deserted concrete strong-point, the lower part of which was already deep in water, a foolish action in any sense. At this juncture a fire-eating bantam, a private from our company, took charge of the situation and literally drove the shelterers away from the dug-out. Despite my normal antipathy to this little braggart, I admired his bravery while wondering how anyone could retain so much initiative in such awful straits. His action on this occasion was not seen by anyone important and therefore not marked down in the records of war, but it was evident to me, despite my ingrained prejudices, why he wore the Belgian Croix de Guerre, awarded to the battalion for some past operation. I remember how the same man, at some time during the following year, openly boasted to all and sundry in the billet that in our next battle he would earn the Victoria Cross. Quite possibly he did; he certainly sacrificed his life.

The horror continued. Shells fell a few paces away, bespattering me with mud. I saw one actually explode among a party on the track just ahead: yet when the fumes cleared away they were all still running, apparently unhurt. The awful mud, though we hardly realised its effectiveness at the time, was completely neutralizing the enemy's efforts to annihilate us. Fortunately he did not think to switch over to shrapnel.

There was something nightmarish and dreamlike in that awful experience. Never before, despite my capacity for fear, had I felt myself for so long in the grip of a terror so absolute. All around us was the continuing threat of instant death. Yet I saw no one fall. I saw men crying, and would have cried myself had I the tears. The company that night was in the grip of a sort of communal terror, a hundred men running like rabbits. I prayed that I would never see its like again.

At length we drew away from the barrage area. Tension began to slacken. We could walk now and regain our breath. Our own guns were replying in good measure and this helped to restore our confidence. The world around throbbed with the discharge of artillery. We were surrounded by ghostly trees that flickered indefinitely in the flashes like a scene at the cinema. The track led down into a narrow vale towards a battery of field guns which were blazing across the route. A taste of peardrops came into my mouth and I smelt the sickly sweetness of tear gas. Foolishly I remembered the little stationer-sweetshop just off the Cromwell Road where, as a youngster, I had bought quarter-pound bags of unrefined fruit sweets for a penny! We fumbled instinctively with our gas helmets but decided not to put them on unless it was absolutely necessary, for we wanted nothing to impede our progress. As we approached nearer and nearer to our guns their shells screamed straight at us to burst, as it seemed, simultaneously with a roar on the enemy positions well behind us, where their dancing bursts lit the sky. For some moments as we passed the guns the whole world seemed to become as black as pitch. Then their servers in gas helmets appeared like leaping demons behind their roaring pieces; even at that cold hour some were stripped to the waist. Such a sight could have been inspiring and, as it was, I felt a glimmer of a thrill run down my spine even though terror still lent wings to my weary limbs.

I now had only two companions, for the company had been scattered far and wide. Shortly we reached the wooden road and were passing through a wood. Occasional shell-bursts in the waste warned us that danger still hung about us, but we had regained self-control. With brief halts on the way we tramped through Hooge and all the way down the Menin Road to Ypres. With all that horror now so far behind the strength which had almost forsaken me was sufficiently reinforced to carry my body to the safety of bivouacs just outside the city, whither our energetic C.Q.M.S. Fail had brought blankets, hot tea and bread to succour the stricken company.

Never had those barely adequate triangular shelters looked so invitingly homelike, as with unbounded gratitude I sank to my knees and thanked God for that deliverance; deliverance from terror rather than death. Others did likewise as they came in, showing that the feeling was communal as well as personal. Never before or again did I see such a thing happen. The miracle of sleep soon fell about me.

The following morning when I pushed my head against the damp roof of the 'bivvy' my immediate feeling was of wonder at my good fortune just to be alive and in a safe place. The camp was already agog with chatter and bustle. Stragglers had been coming in all through the night and the greatest marvel of all was the discovery that there had not been a single casualty during the relief. To me this was incredible and against all the evidence of my eyes. Despite all the sound and fury, the sodden ground had absorbed all the sting of those awful missiles. If only reason had commanded us how brave we could have been under the strain!

After a few jumpy days at Brewery Camp to which we had immediately withdrawn, days during which we were subjected to bombardment by high-velocity shells and aerial torpedoes launched from bomber planes, so that the camp area was ringed with large craters, we went back, by rail from Dickebusch, to the pleasant St. Omer suburb of St. Martin-au-Laert, there to recover from our wounds and to prepare for the next phase of what, in prospect, seemed an unending journey through horror and despair.

Yet if our spirits were subjected to such great stresses that today it seems almost disloyal to recognise the depths into which our despair often led us, it is equally true that we were young and our minds resilient. Days that may well be numbered always seem more precious than those of normal life and we were soon enjoying rural contentment when staying on our farm at St. Omer. We were not yet rejoiced with the knowledge that we had seen the last of the Franco-Belgian sector of the Western Front.

IN CONCLUSION

As we already know, outside events, concerned with the broken morale of one major ally and the utter collapse of another, had fatefully influenced the whole concept and conduct of the Third Battle of Ypres of 1917. Now in the late summer certain new military factors came into the picture.

As one of the alternative operations planned to take place on the Western Front in the event of the Ypres offensive coming to a halt, a major tank assault on the Cambrai sector to the south had been planned. At the very moment when the final battles at Passchendaele were being launched preparations for the Cambrai offensive were involving the assembly of an unusual force of five hundred tanks, as well as the training of infantry divisions specially to co-operate with them. A break-through at a vital point was projected. Aided by fine weather, this new type of assault was launched on 20th November, and the absence of any preliminary artillery bombardment no doubt contributed to the Germans' complete surprise. But after considerable initial success, prematurely heralded as a great victory in Britain, the Germans brought up fresh troops and counter-attacked with great effect on 30th November. A new sort of battle had been initiated, from which the Germans no doubt learned as much as we did, but the attackers had been unable to take advantage of the fluid situation which great tank mobility had placed in their hands. In the end the British held some of the ground captured in the centre of the line, while the Germans on the right had not only taken back all that had been conceded but had pressed forward their front line well behind our original positions, creating a considerable salient.*

The other new event that had the greatest impact on the possibility of continuing the Flanders offensive had been taking place on the Italian Front. In the mountainous terrain on the frontier between Italy and Austria there had been long and bitter fighting between traditional enemies, which had brought heavy losses to both sides. On 17th August the Italians had launched a new offensive on the

* See *Official History*.

Isonzo, eleventh in its series on that particular front, and had made such progress that the Austrians were in danger of being driven from the last foothold on the vital Bainsezza plateau. They appealed to Germany for assistance and, as pressures were weakening on the Eastern Front, this was forthcoming. The German divisions sent as reinforcements took a leading part in a counter-drive at Caporetto which caused the utter collapse of the Italian front and a precipitate retreat towards the open plains of Lombardy. National disaster seemed imminent. As the Germans had acted with decision to keep their ally in the war, so now Britain and France had to act with equal decision, however much it might affect cherished plans in the west. Both Britain and France decided to reinforce the Italians and a comparatively small but effective and well-equipped fighting force was sent. The decision to dispatch the first two British divisions was made on 26th October and the choice fell upon the 23rd and 41st Divisions, which were on the point of being relieved from the line. General Lord Cavan was placed in command and other divisions were to follow: but that is another story. In the event the present author's war experiences were to be given, what might be called in modern phraseology, a new look.

THE FIRST WORLD WAR IN 1917

Chronological Background to the Ypres Battles

January	Year begins with abortive peace soundings and heightening of submarine warfare by German U-boats.
10th Jan. ↓ March	British recommence harassing operations on Somme-Ancre front in France. R.A.F. piece together photographs of Germans' massive new defence line, the *Siegfried Stellung*, known as the Hindenburg Line. Under pressure of General Gough's Fifth Army on Arras front Germans withdraw to new line, after reducing intervening zone to a desert.
February	Unrestricted U-boat warfare constitutes Britain's greatest threat, and pushes the United States towards hostilities.
5th March	In distant Mesopotamia General Maude's British troops press along the Tigris to recapture Baghdad from the Turks on 11th March.
12th March	In Russia—Revolution. Left-wing and moderate Socialists form first Soviet in the Duma building in Petrograd. Provisional government set up under moderate Alexander Kerensky.
15th March	Emperor Nicholas II, last Czar of Russia, abdicates.
2nd April	State of war declared between United States and Germany. U.S. fleet shortly takes part, but an army has to be made.

9th April General Allenby's Third Army launches attack on Arras front, its main success being the capture of Vimy Ridge by the Canadian Corps. Gough's Fifth Army involved on the right. Early in the following month the operations peter out with a total advance of about five miles. Total casualties: British 150,000, Germans over 100,000 and possibly not far short of the British.

16th April General Nivelle launches much-heralded offensive between Reims and Soissons, aiming at a quick break-through in force, but after some initial success the plan miscarries and the operation ends in disaster. Estimated total losses: French 187,000, German 163,000. On 15th May Nivelle is replaced by Pétain.

29th April First instance of 'collective indiscipline' in French Army in Champagne, but the movement does not gain impetus so long as the battle continues. Fortunately the scope of this collapse is kept from the Germans (and also from the British Tommy!). A period of reorganisation and recuperation is needed and under the firm direction of General Pétain and Prime Minister Clemenceau this is to prove successful.

10th May First ships to travel to Britain in convoy leave Gibraltar. The introduction of the convoy system at sea causes the U-boat successes to fall away from their April peak and for the menace to be mastered by the end of the year.

12th May The Tenth Battle of the Isonzo, launched by the Italians, leads to an Allied success with an advance averaging up to two miles, but the total Italian losses are heavy, as they usually have been on their rugged mountain frontiers. In this case they amount to 157,000 as against an Austrian total of

75,000. This was to be offset the following month by an Austrian success in the Trentino.

7th June — **Battle of Messines.** General Plumer's Second Army captures Messines Ridge, which has been reduced by the explosion of nineteen massive mines, and the objectives are taken by the end of the day. The campaign is officially concluded on 14th June. Total British casualties are approximately 25,000 and the Germans 23,000, but for various reasons these figures are not comparable. Thus the scene is set for the great Ypres offensive.

1st July — Russia, still with the Allies, launches her last offensive under General Brusilov against the combined German-Austrian front. This is a complete and disastrous failure. The Russian armies, who have fought so well since 1914 and have given so much, literally dissolve back into Mother Russia!

10th July — The Germans, marking the intention of Messines, make an effective though minor spoiling thrust at Nieuport on the Belgian coast.

31st July — **Third Battle of Ypres** is launched, mainly by Gough's Fifth Army on the left, but supported by Plumer's Second Army on the right. The first operation, known as the **Battle of Pilckem Ridge,** effects a valuable advance of some 3,000 yards and is over within three days. A period of rain supervenes and the next assault, concentrated on the important Gheluvelt plateau on 10th August, has only limited success.

15th Aug. — Canadian Corps launches successful diversionary attack on Hill 70 on the Lens front.

16th Aug. — **Third Battle of Ypres.** Second thrust, delayed by bad weather and known as the **Battle of**

Langemarck, is launched by the Fifth Army, supported on the left by the French First Army. It has only modest success due to the shocking state of the ground, and comes to a standstill on the third day. The main battle is now held up pending re-grouping.

18th Aug. The Italians launch their Eleventh Battle of the Isonzo but, after advancing up to five miles, a halt is called in anticipation of an Austro-German counter-thrust, which fails to materialise.

20th Aug. Marking their progress towards recovery from the mutinies, the French Second Army under General Guillamat launches a successful local blow on the Verdun front.

20th Sept. **Third Battle of Ypres.** General Plumer's Second Army, with the Fifth Army taking a subsidiary part on the north flank, now takes the offensive in the **Battle of the Menin Road**, which, helped by the better weather, is a success and is to be followed:

26th Sept. by the **Battle of Polygon Wood**, and

4th Oct. by the **Battle of Broodseinde**, both equally successful, but now the weather breaks and the next attack:

9th Oct. the **Battle of Poelcapelle** fails. However, Haig hopes still to occupy all the high ground about Passchendaele, now so tantalisingly within his grasp, and continues the campaign:

12th Oct. with the **First Battle of Passchendaele** in which both the Second and Fifth Armies take part and achieve a limited success.

26th Oct. The next series of limited thrusts, known as the **Second Battle of Passchendaele,** is delayed till 26th October and continues into November. During this operation Passchendaele village is captured by the Canadians but when the operations close the Germans still have a foothold on the high ground and the key to the open country has not been attained.

23rd Oct. In the Battle of Malmaison, Pétain with General Maistre's Tenth Army makes another successful advance on the Chemin des Dames front. The French recovery is clearly going on apace.

25th Oct. The Austrians, reinforced by seven German divisions and much equipment, make the long expected offensive under the leadership of the German General von Below and with such effect and surprise as to achieve a complete break-through at Caporetto, driving the sorely tried Italian army into disastrous retreat. For a few days it looks as though Italy is out of the war, but the rout ends way back upon the Piave river. Not only were the Austro-Germans themselves unprepared to exploit such a total success, but news of the arrival of Anglo-French reinforcements from France helped to restore morale—and the Germans felt that their experienced divisions would be more useful back home!

31st Oct. First U.S. Division enters the firing line in France.

31st Oct. General Allenby, now in command of British forces in the Middle East against the Turks, launches a major attack on the Turkish lines in southern Palestine, driving them back and entering Jerusalem on 11th December.

7th Nov. The Bolsheviks seize power and the Revolution is

really on! An armistice is signed with the Germans at Brest-Litovsk on 16th December and the Russians are out of the war.

20th Nov. **Third Battle of Ypres** is officially concluded with considerable success, although a final break-through has not been achieved. Total British losses since 31st July are estimated at 240,000, with the Germans' total about the same.

20th Nov. Successful British tank attack launched by General Byng's Third Army at Cambrai, inaugurating a new type of mechanised warfare. With heavy fighting for Bourlon Wood, the impetus of the attack falls and we are unable to exploit the opportunity created.

30th Nov. At Cambrai a heavy counter-attack by the German Second Army practically wipes out initial British gains and the battlefield subsides under an immense snow blizzard. Each side had about 45,000 casualties: 11,000 Germans and 9,000 Britons are added to the Prisoner of War cages.

31st Dec. So ends a year of mighty global events but with heavy losses on the battle fronts and few spectacular victories. The combatants are now licking their wounds and preparing for the campaigns of 1918, which—except perhaps for the Americans who still lack hard experience—probably looks even more gloomy than any previous New Year since 1914. In their souls at least the Germans realise that it is 1918 or never.

(N.B. Total casualties cover killed, wounded and missing—the latter including those taken prisoner. Comparisons are difficult since the national totals are compiled on different bases, while the British seem to be more complete and reliable than most.)

INDEX